PENGUIN BOOKS

60 Seconds & You're Hired!

With appearances on more than 1,500 TV and radio shows, including *Oprah*, *Dr. Phil*, ABC News, CNN, and NPR, ROBIN RYAN has been called the country's top job search and hiring expert by *The Boston Globe* and the *San Francisco Chronicle*.

She is the bestselling author of *Over 40 & You're Hired*, *Soaring on Your Strengths*, *Winning Resumes*, *Winning Cover Letters*, and *What to Do with the Rest of Your Life*. A frequent contributor to national magazines, she's been featured in *Money*, *Fortune*, *Businessweek*, *Good Housekeeping*, and *Woman's Day*, to name a few. She's appeared in the pages of most major newspapers, including *USA Today*, *The Wall Street Journal*, *The New York Times*, the *Los Angeles Times*, and the *Chicago Tribune*.

A career counselor, Robin Ryan uses her expertise daily, as she helps clients across the country land great jobs, get promotions, change careers, and secure higher salaries. A licensed vocational counselor, she offers telephone consultations to clients worldwide providing interview coaching, resume writing, job search, and career counseling services.

A highly sought-after speaker, she frequently is in front of HR groups, college students, alumni, and association conference attendees. A popular corporate trainer, she teaches numerous employee career development programs each year. She also offers numerous keynotes on job search topics.

Robin holds a master's degree in counseling and education from Suffolk University, a bachelor's degree in sociology from Boston College, and is the former director of counseling services at the University of Washington. You may contact her at (425) 226-0414 or robin@robinryan.com or visit her website at www.RobinRyan.com.

D1016718

6o Seconds & You're Hired!

Robin Ryan

PENGUIN BOOKS

PENGUIN BOOKS

An imprint of Penguin Random House LLC
375 Hudson Street
New York, New York 10014
penguin.com

First published in the United States of America by Impact Publications 1994
Expanded edition published in Penguin Books 2000
Revised edition published 2008
This second revised edition published 2016

LIBRARY OF CONGRESS CATALOGING-IN-PUBLICATION DATA

Names: Ryan, Robin, 1955– author.
Title: 60 seconds and you're hired! / Robin Ryan.
Other titles: Sixty seconds and you're hired
Description: Revised edition. | Santa Barbara : Penguin Books, 2016. |
  Revised edition of the author's 60 seconds and you're hired!, 2008.
Identifiers: LCCN 2015025480 | ISBN 978-0-14-312850-2
Subjects: LCSH: Employment interviewing. | BISAC: BUSINESS & ECONOMICS /
  Careers / General. | BUSINESS & ECONOMICS / Negotiating.
Classification: LCC HF5549.5.I6 R94 2016 | DDC 650.14—dc23 LC record available
at http://lccn.loc.gov/2015025480

Printed in the United States of America
15   17   19   20   18   16   14

Set in Janson Text

*To my husband Steve, my son Jack, Mom, and Dad
And in memory of my former secretary, Wanda Bartel*

Can This Book
Help You Get Hired?

You will not land the job unless you excel in the interview. And you are not likely to secure the best possible salary unless you are skilled in salary negotiations. My clients have tried every technique and have successfully used the answers in this book to land terrific jobs. If you find marketing yourself difficult, be comforted to know that it does not come easily to anyone. Yet thousands of job hunters have read this book and quickly learned what to say, what not to say, and how to answer the tough questions. They learned the best ways to sell themselves in interviews. And the results speak for themselves— they got the job! That's the reason I think this will be a valuable resource to help you land the position you want.

I spend most of my workdays advising clients or talking to hiring managers. I've given hundreds of speeches and appeared on many TV and radio shows to share the insights in this book, even discussing it on *Oprah*. I care about giving you the best possible advice, which is why I have updated this book to make sure you will be ready to wow any employer you talk to. This updated edition contains a great deal of new content with a new chapter, new facts and research, as well as additional hiring strategies and client-proven techniques. It is also concise, so that you can read it in its entirety the night before your interview. This new edition contains 132 answers that have been used in real interviews where my clients faced employers who asked the same difficult questions.

Preparation is the key to your success. Everything you need to know to excel in your next interview is covered in the pages that follow. Read on, and you can be assured you'll do the best job possible when you're in the hot seat.

I continually hear success story after success story about how this book has helped job hunters land great jobs. I'm convinced it will be as effective for you as it has been for so many others—so do let me know when you get your new job.

To your success—

Robin Ryan

Acknowledgments

I am continually grateful for being able to play a small role in helping others improve their lives. I send a big thank-you to every career-counseling client I have worked with and to the numerous job hunters who've attended my seminars. Helping others reach their career dreams is why I wrote this book. In 2012 though, my own career got interrupted. I was diagnosed with breast cancer and it took me eighteen months to deal with the harsh treatments and recover. It was a horrible experience—one I hope you don't go through. God played a saving role and I'm in remission and cancer free as I write this. As my supportive friend Sherry Holt says, "Robin, you still have many people to help."

I've had many big moments because of this book—being on *Oprah*, touring the United States with colleges such as RIT and Michigan, countless book signings—that kick-started my life as an author. Above all, I am a career counselor and have dedicated my days to helping people find fulfilling jobs. Hearing that they *landed* their desired job always makes my day.

There are a few important people to thank. Some are in other editions, but these people stand out. From Penguin: my original editor Jane von Mehren, for believing in and endorsing this book so wholeheartedly; Maureen Donnelly, vice president of publicity (who sadly passed away last year), was a champion of authors and always supported me in my efforts with the media; Patrick Nolan, who sold many copies of this book and was quick to foster a new edition; Matt Klise, who makes sure everything gets taken care of.

I have created many relationships with terrific hiring managers and HR people who freely share their time and expertise with me. One woman deserves special recognition, Tracy White, a senior director of HR. She started my seminar business years ago when she first hired me to teach job-hunting skills. Her continued support, endorsement, and friendship have been an important contribution to my career.

Over the years, several assistants have worked on this book and its updated editions. I'm grateful to Dawnelle Thompson, Cindy Jackson, and Sylvia Coppock for their help. It was Wanda Bartel who aided me as I wrote my last edition. Wanda was my secretary for nearly five years and also my dear friend. Wanda died in 2012 from cancer herself. She was a special, fun-loving lady and I miss her very much.

Dee Murphy has become someone I just can't survive without. She is an extraordinary assistant and a kind, wonderful human being. Leslie Ault helps me in my office and home—I sure appreciate all she does.

My husband Steven, my beloved son Jack, and our adorable Westie dog Duffy are truly the light of my life.

Some good fortune comes purely from destiny. I am ever so lucky to have parents that raised me to believe that with determination, dedication, and enthusiasm you can achieve any goal you can dream of.

Contents

60 Seconds *&* You're Hired!

Believing in yourself is the starting point. Effectively communicating your abilities to others is the necessity.

CHAPTER I

Why 60 Seconds?

"We would like you to come in for an interview." Those wonderful words are what every job hunter wants to hear. Once they are said, a vision of landing the job starts to form in the job hunter's mind. When you get that call you hang up the phone, excited and pleased that your resume has gotten you this far.

On the other end of the phone sits the employer who decided to call you in for an interview. Three thoughts are running through his mind: *Can you do the job? Will you do the job? Will you work out in their organization so they can manage you?* The employer is worried. It's hard to find a person who'll be a good fit. The workload is piling up; the pressure is on to make a good hiring decision. The employer hopes that you'll be "the one." He reiterates the important job duties he needs done. He's feeling anxious, hopeful, and skeptical all at once. He's praying that you have the skills to do the work.

For the employer, hiring is a difficult task. Mistakes can be very costly. Employee turnover often costs three times the person's salary, when adding the loss of work, expense of errors, and training a new person. The employer wants to find the right person—quickly. He looks for someone who can and will perform the job well. He looks for an answer to the problem of whom to hire.

There are several compelling reasons why the 60-seconds approach is the ideal way to get your points across and convince an employer to hire you.

Attention Span

In today's fast-paced world, it's become much harder to get people's attention. Twitter messages have only 140 characters, texts are brief, advertisements keep getting shorter. Verbose, lengthy answers, where job hunters babble on and on when answering interview questions, bore the interviewer into not hiring them. Nervousness and lack of preparation often result in long, rambling, erroneous, or never-ending answers.

The most effective way to capture attention is to use your enthusiasm to answer each question succinctly in a concise, brief manner. Never use more than 60 seconds on any answer.

Are They Listening?

Job hunters are amazed to learn that interviewers can ask them an hour's worth of questions and never hear any of the answers. Why? Because they aren't listening. They are tired, distracted, and bored and feel the candidate is the wrong choice—that he or she can't do the job. When you get your point across in 60 seconds or less, you increase the odds that the person will listen. When you add specifics of how you've accomplished the needed tasks before, show support materials and work examples, and add vocal variety and enthusiasm to your answers, the employer starts to wake up and take notice. And when you put into practice two proven techniques you'll learn in this book—

the 5 Point Agenda and the 60 Second Sell—the whole process takes on a new shape. The employer begins to get *excited* that she may have found the right person for the job—YOU!

The World Is Full of Sound Bites

The media has filled our world with short, concise commercials that quickly get their points across. News reports use the same principles, limiting stories to one- to three-minute segments. We are all conditioned to these speedy communication tools. During a job interview, utilizing the right words that effectively get your message across concisely will build the employer's confidence that you can do the job.

Your Verbal Business Card

The 60 Second Sell is your basic tool to spark an employer's interest. This 60-second calling card will summarize your skills, abilities, and previous experience in a well-thought-out fashion that will immediately make the employer want to listen. The 60 Second Sell is a proven shortcut to your success. Client upon client has reported it was the best job-search technique they'd ever used. It's easy to create and easy to implement. Once you've learned this technique, your interviews will be greatly improved because you will be able to do the most important thing necessary to land a job—get the employer to listen to you while you're telling him exactly how you can perform his job.

In the end, what does any

work mean to me?

That I have done my best,

excelled where I could,

taken risks,

and made a difference by being here.

CHAPTER 2

5 Point Agenda

The 5 Point Agenda is a method by which you can focus your interview on your strengths, break through the monotony and disinterest, and get the employer to listen. It is a hiring strategy created to focus on the needs of the employer and the job to be done. The 5 Point Agenda is a predetermined analysis in which you select your five most marketable points and repeatedly illustrate these points throughout the interview process. It is this repetition and reiteration of exactly how you'll meet her needs that allows the employer to remember something about you. My clients have tested this interview approach with the following results:

- It made interview preparation easier.
- They were highly rated by everyone who interviewed them.
- The five points seemed to be all that was remembered.
- They credited the 5 Point Agenda and the 60 Second Sell as being the two techniques that secured the job offer.

Job hunters are often amazed to learn that an interviewer can ask you questions for an entire hour and not hear one word you've said. He may be bored, frustrated, or unimpressed with your image within the first few answers. After he's interviewed several people, all the candidates begin to blend together. I experience this when I hire people, and countless other employers continually confirm this fact. The 5 Point Agenda quickly captures an employer's interest because you are constantly emphasizing exactly how you *can* do the job right from the start.

The Formula: Creating Your Strategy

Examine your previous experience. Write out the major responsibilities for each job you've held. Note any special accomplishments. Zero in on your important work strengths—those abilities where you excel and are most productive.

Then, check with your contacts and use your network to get as much background as possible about the employer, the company, and the position's needs. Many times, your contacts will point out the very aspects that must make up your 5 Point Agenda. Other times, there will be little information available and you will need to guess based on your general knowledge about performing the job.

After reviewing the employer's and position's needs, determine which of your abilities and which aspects of your experience will be most important *to the employer*. Then create your 5 Point Agenda, selecting each point to build a solid picture emphasizing how you can do the best job.

Five Examples

Let's examine these 5 Point Agendas that clients used during the interview process to land their new jobs.

General Counsel/Chief Legal Counsel

Fearing a layoff after a merger was completed with her current employer, this talented lady found an interesting position to go after with a large healthcare organization that would challenge her. The competition was stiff. Here is her 5 Point Agenda:

- Point 1: Twenty years of experience in billion-dollar healthcare organizations.
- Point 2: Known for delivering notable cost savings and operational improvements.
- Point 3: Development of a new physicians' foundation that delivered millions in new revenues.
- Point 4: Responsible for building a much-improved relationship with the organization's physicians that has helped us grow.
- Point 5: Exceeds goals and expectations.

Software Engineer

This client wanted to take the few years of experience he'd gotten at a smaller IT company and move to a popular tech organization where there is a lot of competition for any job. Networking helped him land an interview. His 5 Point Agenda was:

- Point 1: Four years of software engineering experience.
- Point 2: Data analysis was his major job function.
- Point 3: Had C# and C++ programming experience.
- Point 4: Supervisor constantly said he had excellent report writing skills.
- Point 5: Trained new team members.

Human Resources Director

This company wanted to find a progressive HR partner to lead their organization. They needed a strategic leader. The client had heard about the position from a friend at an HR conference and wanted to go after the job. Her 5 Point Agenda needed to stress her achievements.

- Point 1: Award-winning human resources leader.
- Point 2: Providing strategic direction for organization that was recently named a national best-places-to-work company.
- Point 3: Strong entrepreneurial drive was responsible for delivering new programs, HR systems, and major policy enhancements.
- Point 4: A strategic and operational business partner working closely with top executives.
- Point 5: Exceeds goals and expectations.

Program Coordinator

Making a career change seemed overwhelming, but this math and science teacher wanted to move on into an area where he could earn more money. It was a position in a large company needing a program coordinator that he targeted. His 5 Point Agenda included:

- Point 1: Six years of experience as a math and science teacher.
- Point 2: Extensive program coordination expertise.
- Point 3: Organized numerous events.
- Point 4: Technical oral and written communications skills.

- Point 5: Highly productive individual contributor and successfully worked in a collaborative team environment.

Graphic and Web Designer

It was this client's dream job that she went after. A promotion, this highly attractive job was in Europe. The internal competition was very high, and the hiring manager elected to allow external candidates to apply also. Her 5 Point Agenda was:

- Point 1: Fifteen years of experience for two Fortune 500 companies.
- Point 2: Very creative with extensive portfolio of original graphic concepts and published works.
- Point 3: Complex experience with manuals and webpages—a key noted job function.
- Point 4: Excellent writing and editing skills.
- Point 5: Fluent in Spanish, French, Italian.

Summary

Before every job interview, you will customize your 5 Point Agenda to reflect the responsibilities of the job as well as the company's goals and objectives. These five points are your basic building blocks to answer the interviewer's questions. You'll want to re-stress each of these points whenever the opportunity presents itself. The message the employer will hear is that you have the ability to perform and do well in the job—and it will give your prospective boss confidence in hiring you.

*You'll never know
what you can achieve
until you try.
Just never, ever give up.*

CHAPTER 3

60 Second Sell

The 60 Second Sell is a tool that helps you target your skills to meet the employer's needs. It allows you to summarize your most marketable strengths in a brief and concise manner. Successful job hunters have found that the 60 Second Sell is the most influential tool they used during the interview process. They praised the tool for several reasons:

- It was effective in capturing the employer's attention.
- It provided excellent, concise answers to tricky questions.
- It was very easy to use.
- It was a great way to end an interview.

The 60 Second Sell is a 60-second statement that you customize for each interview and that summarizes and links together your 5 Point Agenda. You will want to put the points of your 5 Point Agenda into an order that allows you to present them in the most logical and effective manner. When you link the ideas into sentences, they should be spoken in 60 seconds or less. Once memorized, this statement will be easy for you to recall and use during the interview.

When to Use It

Most interviews are over before they ever really get started. What should you do to avoid this trap? Immediately capture the employer's attention and get him tuned in to you as a true top-notch candidate. You need to open the interview by using your 60 Second Sell. Typically the first question you are asked in an interview is *Tell me about yourself*. In an interview I recently conducted, I got a twenty-minute answer. After the first minute or two, the prospect totally lost my attention. Had the person answered with a 60 Second Sell, he might have started the interview by grabbing my attention and keeping it. Questions such as *Tell me about yourself* require a brief summary noting your most marketable skills, not a life story.

Another question to which your 60 Second Sell is the perfect answer: *Why should I hire you?* This question is asking you to convince the employer to hire you. Other applicable inquiries include: *What are your strengths? What makes you think you are qualified for this job? What makes you think you will succeed in this position? Why do you want this job?* These questions offer you an excellent way to stress your 5 Point Agenda (your most marketable skills) using your 60 Second Sell.

The 60 Second Sell is effective because it demonstrates your strengths and illustrates how you will fill the employer's needs. That is the key to its success, and yours.

Five Examples

To clearly understand how your 5 Point Agenda is linked and becomes your 60 Second Sell, let's continue with our five earlier examples; here is how the candidates took their 5 Point

Agenda and linked the points together to summarize them and create their 60 Second Sell.

General Counsel/Chief Legal Counsel

"I have a proven track record serving as the in-house general counsel with twenty years of experience directing the legal department and corporate governance for billion-dollar healthcare organizations. I'm a creative problem solver known for delivering notable cost savings and operational improvements. My most significant accomplishment in the last two years was the development of a new physicians' foundation that delivered millions in new revenues. I am a key adviser to executives, department heads, and staff on business and legal issues. When I took over my current position there was great animosity between the administration and the organization's doctors. I worked very hard as the key executive responsible for building a much-improved relationship with the organization's physicians that has helped us grow and bring in millions in new revenue. I'm known as an innovative thinker and strategist, and I always strive to exceed goals and expectations."

Software Engineer

"I'm a software engineer with four years of experience delivering notable results. I've created new software and embedded systems via C++ and C# in manufacturing airplane electronics. My current job requires a lot of collaboration with other technical teams as we conduct data analysis that I pull from global databases. I have also trained new team members and engineers on our data retrieval process. My supervisor has stated that I have excellent technical writing skills based on the comprehensive reports and training manuals I've produced that have wide

among vendors. These skills and experience will
to quickly contribute to your organization and be a
ductive part of your team."

Human Resources Director

"I've been an award-winning human resources leader with fifteen years of experience providing strategic direction. I'm proud to share that my current employer was recently named a national best-places-to-work company. I am a global thinker who contributed to the company's success as a strategic and operational business partner, and we have cut attrition by 60%. I display a strong entrepreneurial drive at work. I have been responsible for delivering new programs, HR systems, and major policy enhancements. My CEO has repeatedly recognized me for my innovative leadership that often exceeds goals and expectations."

Program Coordinator

"I have six years of work experience as a math and science teacher that includes an extensive program coordination background. In my past job, I have successfully planned, organized, and supervised numerous events and activities. I'm highly analytical with superior technical oral and written communications skills. Highly productive and efficient, I excel as both an individual contributor and also working in a collaborative team environment."

Graphic and Web Designer

"I'd bring fifteen years of visual design and technical writing experience, having worked for two Fortune 500 companies. I'm highly creative. In my past positions, I've delivered original concepts producing sophisticated graphics and illustrations for the manufacturing and technical departments. I've primarily worked on complex manuals and webpages. I not only have excellent writing and editing skills in English but am completely fluent in Spanish, French, and Italian. I've always produced creative results and feel that I would be able to make significant contributions to meet your team's goals too."

Summary

Both the 60 Second Sell and the 5 Point Agenda must be customized and created for *each* interview. They may vary slightly or greatly based on what you determine to be that employer's most important needs and your most marketable abilities to meet those needs. These tools allow you to take control of the interview and get the employer to recognize the kinds of abilities and contributions you will bring to the job and the organization.

Be delighted at the prospect of
a new day, a new possibility,
and a new page of your life that is yet unwritten
and can be filled with anything
you wish to make happen.

CHAPTER 4

Hiring Trends

Billions of dollars are lost every year by U.S. companies from bad hires. BILLIONS! One out of every five hires will be regretted and/or terminated. Tony Hsieh, the CEO of Zappos, a $1.2 billion online shoe company, stated in a TV interview that over the course of its rapid paced growth, hiring mistakes and bad hires cost the company more than $100 million. The costs of poor hires and expenses caused by turnover errors, productivity loss, and recruiting new people are much higher than many people think. *Forbes* reported that for entry-level employees, it costs between 30% and 50% of their annual salary to replace them. For mid-level employees that amount is upwards of 150% of their annual salary to replace a departed person. For high-level or highly specialized employees, the cost to find, train, and get up to speed is reported to be 400% of their annual salary.

Hiring is of paramount concern to everyone from the CEO down to the manager who makes the choice of who gets the job. In the past, an employer would seek out an employee to "fill the job description." Today, in response to the rapidly changing marketplace, organizations—large, medium, and small—now compete globally for their business. To better meet the needs of tomorrow's workplace, employers hire nimble employees today who can maximize productivity, advance their own personal development, and still be of value to an employer tomorrow.

A few notable hiring trends that you must recognize:

- An emphasis on finding more productive and adaptable workers.
- Companies continue to experience increasing difficulty in finding *qualified* candidates to hire and are either willing to wait to find the right person or forced to hire someone and spend the time to train them. The Society of Human Resources Management reports that 49% of organizations are now forced to spend money to extensively train a new hire to be able to perform the job.
- Efforts continue to streamline costs, utilize technology, and lay off employees—many who have been with their organization more than ten years.
- Internal promotions—the ones you apply for and interview for—are on the rise.
- Companies actively search LinkedIn profiles to uncover employed potential job candidates and actively recruit these identified people to apply for their job openings. More qualified candidates are being found and hired this way.
- Strong ethics and integrity are now sought-after traits by employers (in the wake of too many corporate scandals). Over 50% of companies report they actively search social media on an applicant before they make a job offer. That number is growing daily.
- The number-one complaint from hiring managers is that candidates display poor communication skills, such as inarticulate answers and vague accounts of past

experience, never mentioning any personal accomplishments or results they have achieved in past positions.

- The crackdown on lying is commonplace, with increased reference checks and post-hire firings if false information is uncovered.
- Interview etiquette is a necessary concern for employers. Dress, image, and personal presentation are undergoing greater scrutiny than ever before.
- The interview process is seeing a rise in testing prior to hiring. This may include competency, management style, personality, and software usage testing, as well as on-the-job assessment and drug testing.
- More and more organizations now use situational questions during their interview process.
- In addition to experience when hiring, employers look for future potential, demonstration of past initiative, and a "success attitude."

Salary Trends

As a long-term employee, you typically can expect to receive a 2–5% raise annually. The largest raises come when you change employers, move up, and negotiate your new salary, which has often proved to be 15–20% higher. *Forbes* recently stated that the loyal employee who remains over many years will earn 50% less than the proactive employee who changes jobs several times over his or her working lifetime. For a mid-level person, a professional or manager, that could amount to between $500,000 and $1,000,000 in lost wages you could have earned had you managed your career more correctly and moved on to new employers, better jobs, and higher salaries.

Among other recent salary trends:

- Employers are showing more latitude and willingness to negotiate salary and benefits, most often improving initial offers when asked.
- The biggest raises come when changing jobs and moving from one employer to another.

Where People Want to Work

Fast-paced companies like Google and Apple have become the popular organizations new workers flock to. There they have found a sense of accomplishment, many opportunities to shine, and salary packages offering top dollar for their skills. Additionally, they offer many people the opportunity to move up along the way. Many popular employers look at the skill set and, more important, the "future potential" of would-be employees, assessing their past performances as well as their flexibility, adaptability, and job attitudes. The competition to land one of these highly sought-after jobs is staggering. Microsoft claims to receive more than three million resumes a year—that's competition!

Individuals now seek out satisfying and personally rewarding work and relish contributing personal accomplishments to their organization. They want to be recognized and appreciated. In the future, workers will put even more emphasis on finding satisfaction in their jobs. The top reason that people change positions today is dissatisfaction and feeling disengaged—it's a powerful trend that employers are responding to.

Many workers are now searching for employers with a mission they can believe in. Whether it is to fight for a political cause, to safeguard the environment, or to help other people overcome life's problems, they select jobs and employers because they feel they can make an important difference by working there. Meaningful work and helping others—not salary or stock options—is their daily incentive. They want to make the world, or at least the part they live in, a better place. Landing these jobs remains challenging because so many people seek these opportunities.

Overall, competition for the most desirable and lucrative positions is, and will remain, stiff. To land one, superior interview skills are indispensable.

Employers' Changing Needs

Global competitiveness, technology enhancements, mergers, acquisitions, outsourcing, and the Internet are reshaping the way employers do business. Restructuring and layoffs are commonplace, and, ironically, at the same time these companies are firing, they are actively recruiting new key people to help them move forward.

Today, many employers report a mismatch between the skills their company needs and those its current workers offer. The movement is toward looking for people with more broadly based skills and documented strengths—adaptable learners who have demonstrated the ability to grow into future jobs. Hiring now takes on a more futurist attitude. Companies not only seek experience but now hire people for their aptitude (what they are able to do) and their attitude (what they are willing to do). Most need productive workers who can fit into a team-based organization, since most large companies use teams to drive the work and meet corporate goals. Hiring adaptable people is critical whether a company employs 20 people or 200,000. Organizations now hire managers who show leadership strength as people who can achieve results. Nationally, emerging companies, nonprofits, Fortune 500, small businesses, and governmental agencies are all responding to a need for an adaptable workforce. Therefore the desire to find and hire the "ideal worker persona" is the most significant of all hiring changes.

Cultivating the Ideal Worker Persona

Employers often stereotype people. An older worker is typically viewed as less driven, no longer having as much innovation, energy, or enthusiasm and possessing weaker computer skills. Millennial workers are known for their fascination with their phones and seem to have expert tech skills, but are often viewed as entitled and loyal only to themselves and want to be promoted quickly and frequently. Working parents can get pegged as being preoccupied and/or unreliable because of kids and their personal problems. Laid-off workers may be viewed as somewhat tainted and/or of less value because they are not employed. To set yourself apart from any stereotyped group, learn to project what all employers desire: the "ideal worker persona." These are quick learners, adaptable, flexible, and willing to try to succeed at new tasks. They take their own professional development to the highest level possible and excel at core strengths.

Attitude and some effort are all that is needed to develop this highly desired persona. In fact, taking this new, proactive approach to performing your job is not difficult. Workers of any age can develop these traits that will increase their career potential by making them more appealing to employers. Job security and work longevity now depend on the worker—her talents, skills, and measurable achievements. It is your perceived potential and career identity that ensures you'll always be able to find a new job. No company offers a permanent guarantee of work anymore. Today, savvy workers always keep the door open for an opportunity to move to a better position.

Here are the keys to developing the "ideal worker persona" skill set:

- **Choose a field and type of work you love.** It'll be a great deal easier. Passion gives purpose and ignites interest in continuing to learn and grow.
- **Develop your strengths into a top-notch skill set.** Innate talents give rise to increased success and better performance on the job. These strengths are easier for you to use and will develop more quickly, so applying them in your job is the best way to stand out.
- **Advance key communication and computer skills.** These are essential in most jobs. Excellent writing is critical in each email or report you send. Coaching, leading, teaching—all require solid oral communication ability. Computer software must be learned, and the better you know it, the more productive you will be. These are skills you can strive to improve daily.
- **Be a lifelong learner.** Read and stay ahead in your field. Improving your skills and diversifying them is critical to lifetime success and employment. It also makes you more enthusiastic, a better problem solver, and thus more appealing during the job interview.
- **Go to work with a "success attitude."** Focus your attitude on productivity and constantly look for ways to save money, save time, and improve the company as well as your own individual performance. Wasting less time socializing, gossiping, or doing personal things while at work makes you efficient. It also helps contribute to a team effort and congenial workplace where employees are able to get more done during hours on the job.
- **Be flexible and adaptable.** This means finding solutions, making suggestions, solving problems, and

being willing to show initiative and to take on new
projects, tasks, or responsibilities. Show that you are
willing to become the worker the employer needs today
and to grow into the one he'll need tomorrow.

Once you've cultivated these traits, success at job interviews
and promotions will result because you will be seen as the ideal
worker the employer wants to hire and keep.

Smile your best smile,

wear your best clothes,

and you will feel like you

can conquer anything.

CHAPTER 5

Interview Etiquette

W*ebster's New World College Dictionary* defines the word *etiquette* as "The manners established by convention as acceptable or required in society and business."

If you are uncertain of the proper image, manners, and behavior to display to potential employers, and want a competitive edge over other candidates, here are some useful guidelines for what's essential to excel in your next job interview.

Dress Up!

Sloppy, sexy, sluttish, wrinkled, or filthy clothes have no place at work, explains HR director Tracy Brown. Today, too many people—young and old alike—have lost touch with the essentials of appropriate business dress. Most companies have a business casual workplace environment, and to a few people that seems to mean anything goes. Not true! Companies are quite serious about who they hire. Remember that your interview is a test to review your professionalism and seriousness about the job.

In the first ten seconds of meeting you, the interviewer

makes a decision about whether you look right for the job. If your personal presentation is inappropriate, you've lost the position without saying a word. Therefore, dress up but be conservative. Business suits, shirts, ties, and blazers for men. Suits—jacket and skirt or matching pantsuit—for women. Carry only a briefcase or leather notebook or purse so you always have one free hand.

Neatness is as important as appropriate attire. Shine your shoes. Clothes should be clean, pressed, and fit well. No tears or missing buttons. Shower. Men's hair should be combed and their nails clean and trimmed. Women need a professional hairstyle, and manicured nails should be freshly done. Use a light hand applying makeup. Skip cologne. Men, watches, no necklaces or bracelets, and one ring work best. Women, simple jewelry that isn't distracting is appropriate.

Display Good Manners During Meals

Meals often relax and encourage candidates to chat and say things that hurt their candidacy. Keep in mind that this is still an interview—you are not speaking off the record.

In the restaurant, select an entrée that is easy to eat (not barbecued ribs, or other drippy or messy finger foods). Don't lick your fingers. Do not order the most expensive items on the menu. And avoid alcohol. You need to remain sharp.

Never monopolize the conversation and don't curse or tell crude or sexual jokes. Employers are evaluating your communication skills and how you would interact at company functions or client meetings. Ask a lot of questions about the company, the duties of the job, and immediate challenges. A good, conversational question is to ask the interviewer how he or she likes the company and why it's a good place to work. Throughout the meal, continually sell yourself and your ability to do the job. Be brief with personal information, and do not mention family obligations such as coaching your child's team or other time-consuming things that may cut into your work time.

Employers will notice how you treat others, especially the server. Be polite. Remember to say "please" and "thank you." In an upscale restaurant with extensive silverware, start at the outside and work your way in. Your salad fork will be on the far left; your entrée fork will be next to it. Your dessert spoon and fork will be above your plate. Your water glass will be on the right and your bread plate will be on the left. Put your napkin on your lap once everyone is seated. Throughout the meal, keep your elbows off the table, sit up straight, and do not talk with your mouth full. It's customary for the employer to pay the tab, so do not offer to do so.

Practice Your Handshake, Eye Contact, and Nonverbal Communication

Greet the interviewer with a smile, and offer a firm handshake. Nothing creates a poorer impression than a weak handshake with a couple of fingers. Eye contact is crucial—it conveys confidence and says that you and your message are believable. During the meeting, be sure not to sit there stoically with a blank face. You will fail to appear "real" or even interested and will come across as robotic, boring, and dull. Be yourself, smile, and maintain eye contact with the person who has asked the question. Use vocal intonations to make your point so you'll seem personable. Movements, gestures, posture, and facial expressions are an important part of your overall performance. A sincere smile sends a warm, confident message—so smile frequently.

Arrive on Time

There is no exception to this rule. Many employers feel that if you're late for the interview, you may never show up on time for your job. Need I say more? Get directions, know how to get there, and give yourself more than enough time so that you will arrive early. Wait, collect your thoughts, and then open the employer's door about five minutes early.

Use People's Names

Introduce yourself as soon as you arrive, stating who your appointment is with and at what time. If the receptionist is wearing a name tag, greet her by name. When you are introduced to the interviewer, or multiple interviewers, use their names in your greeting and also as you depart. People love hearing their names, so remember to use them—sparingly. Too much seems phony. Be sure to ask who your prospective boss would be so you know who the main decision maker is.

Don't Brag, Lie, or Speak Badly About Anyone

Selling yourself effectively means giving examples that substantiate your claims. Exaggeration or lying often comes from weak candidates who think they can fool the interviewer. Most employers *will* check out your claims, and many a candidate who deceives to get hired is surprised when they are later caught and fired! Just don't do it. Bragging is often a major turnoff—avoid it—and most people don't like name-dropping either. It's disrespectful to run down former bosses or employers, and doing so will reflect badly on you, not them. Therefore, do not say anything negative. It would be better to simply say nothing at all.

Impress Them: Handwrite Your Thank-you Note

Employers can be influenced once you have left the door. A thank-you note can tip the hand in your favor, if the decision is between you and someone else. The employer believes a person who really wants the job is likely to perform better on the job. Your note should be written on a card with the words "Thank You" gracing its front with a professional, businesslike design. These can be found at a local drugstore or card shop. Jot down a few lines, thanking the interviewer for the opportunity and reiterating one or two of the strengths you would bring as a "valuable contributor to their team."

Typed notes or letters feel like office mail and are discarded. Emails are immediately forgotten. Handwritten notes (print if your writing is not legible) are a *personal* communication, and their rareness nowadays will make yours stand out. This is an opportunity to demonstrate the extra effort you put into your work and to set yourself apart. So handwrite your notes and mail them within twenty-four hours of the meeting.

*Success comes from thinking
and believing in yourself
and your abilities
to aim higher and do more.*

CHAPTER 6

The Job Promotion Interview

Promoting from within is a common practice at many companies. Your knowledge of company policies, practices, and procedures is seen as a big plus. It is a *fatal* error to assume that you will automatically be moved up. Too many people have lost the job by making this assumption. Larger companies will make you apply for any new jobs you seek. You often go through a screening process before they narrow down whom they plan to talk to in person.

You must treat this critical interview as if you were going to a new organization. That is exactly how my client, a chief financial officer, approached the bid to become her company's new CEO after her boss announced his retirement. One major problem stood in her way. The departing CEO did not support her goal of moving into the top position. Only with a carefully developed presentation of her skills and abilities would the board of directors view her as the prime candidate.

She entered with a great resume and cover letter, and we had polished her interview skills and planned out her hiring strategy. She worked hard to explain her leadership ability and did her very best to prepare. She spent many hours considering the company's future, its challenges, and how she could best lead it. Yet the lack of support from the current leader gave her big doubts about landing this job. All the research, practice answering questions, and role-playing paid off. She proved her value and did, indeed, become the organization's new CEO.

John called in a panic when he was told his department was being eliminated. This thirty-eight-year-old manager had been with his Fortune 500 company since college graduation. He was encouraged to apply inside the company. I recommended he network heavily with anyone he knew inside the organization. That led to several conversations on potential upcoming openings. Within two months he had three interviews for new jobs inside the company outside his division. He worried about the interviews because he didn't know any of the interviewers and had not interviewed in seventeen years. We crafted his five selling points, worked on answering questions, and role-played. He landed all three jobs and selected the one he liked the best. He also got a nice 10% raise and was relieved and happy to find a new job so quickly.

The key factor for inside interviews is to do the research. Find out what colleagues at other companies and competitors are doing in the job you hope to land. Read the trade journals and search the Internet for industry news. Most important, be able to clearly define how you'd perform, and bring in a few ideas to discuss on that issue. Bring samples of your work that illustrate your ability to do the new job. Be able to give clear examples of your experience and how and what you'd do to improve the productivity in the job you seek. Many internal candidates lose the job by failing to do this homework.

Craft your 5 Point Agenda and 60 Second Sell carefully. Offer examples of your initiative. Discuss how you have taken on new tasks and are flexible and adaptable.

If this potential promotion is a move into management, discuss any volunteer or team projects you've headed up. They want evidence that you can firmly and effectively manage the work of others. Mention if you have trained any new hires or led any projects, teams, or committees. Be sure to tell them about any leadership classes you have taken.

Sometimes both internal and external candidates are considered. Management is looking at what others can do. If you are an internal candidate, stress that you'll bring new ideas while not taking six months to get to know the company the way an outsider would—you'll be productive from day one. Comment on two or three immediate problems or concerns you'll tackle, defining the solutions you'd use.

In some situations, a long-term employee takes on the "acting job"—for example, acting director—while a search is under way. This often means the organization was not comfortable offering you the job outright. Use this interim time to do your best, but know that with no real authority from management your results may be minimal. Fresh blood often seems to be management's solution, since "acting" employees typically aren't the ideal selection from the start, which can explain why the company is doing a broad search (though some governmental agencies and nonprofits are required to advertise as well as consider internal people). Be prepared for this interview. Show that you can do it by bringing good, leave-behind work samples and an outline of how you would perform the job going forward.

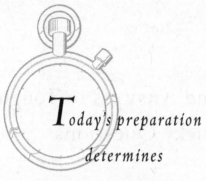

Today's preparation determines tomorrow's achievements.

60-Second Answers to Tough, Tricky Questions

There are four key components to successfully answering interview questions:

- Advance preparation
- Giving short, concise, specific answers that never exceed 60 seconds
- Demonstrating ability to perform the job
- Exhibiting traits of the ideal worker persona

The key to answering even the toughest questions is to think about them and prepare answers before the interview.

In order to help you prepare, I've answered 128 tough, tricky questions here (plus 5 others in chapter 8), including the typical ones you'll most likely be asked. Knowing how to answer the employer's questions is vital to your success. Your self-confidence is dependent on knowing you can effectively answer questions that demonstrate to the employer that you can do the job. I'll show where to use examples that reiterate your 5 Point Agenda and where to use your 60 Second Sell.

Employers know that nervousness can cause job hunters to babble endlessly. Demonstrate your self-confidence and retain their interest with short, effective answers. Too often job hunters answer a question, pause, get nervous, and add more information, which takes away from the initial answer. Monosyllabic answers are not effective either. Strive to be concise but also complete. Short, concise answers that encourage a conversation and exchange of information are ideal.

Whenever possible, give a specific work example of how you've operated in the past. Employers want assurance that you'll be able to do the job. Offering explanations that include examples of how you solved a key problem, saved money, or added to the bottom line can be very influential. While not all skills or accomplishments can be quantified, many can, so practice sharing them. It's wise to have specific examples to point out any positive results you've achieved, whether it's reorganizing the filing system or trimming production costs through some process change. Examples can also include the results of volunteer jobs and outside activities. These are skills you have acquired and will use on the job.

Whenever possible, use descriptive words that paint a picture of how well you've performed the task in the past. Also include how willing you are to take on new tasks as needed. Your willingness to learn and be a value-added asset to the company, keeping its needs in mind, will make you a very appealing candidate.

Research the Company and Potential Boss

Even the smallest companies have a website. Many large organizations have hundreds of pages about their organization. When called for an interview, inquire about the names of the company's and department's websites. Write down the name of the potential boss and ask the caller to spell the name so it's correct.

Do your homework. Go read about the company. Learn what its specialties are and any new products or services it's offering. Check with your network to gather any insider information you can find that will aid you in shaping your answers. Additionally, go to www.glassdoor.com. On this website, select the Interview tab and type in the company name. People who have interviewed at this organization often list some questions they were asked and note some of their interview experience. For example, several people stated that one popular Fortune 100 company asks every interviewee two or three questions on diversity and the role it plays in their work. That was a great tip, since most people would be unprepared for that type of question.

Go to LinkedIn.com and look up the potential boss and get some revealing clues about this decision maker. What does his or her page say about them? Are they endorsed? What do the recommendations say? You may learn a lot by taking this extra step.

Behavioral Interviewing and Situational Questions

Behavioral interviewing techniques are becoming very common. This style of interviewing asks you to give specific examples of positive and negative work situations. Job hunters frequently find these questions very difficult. The interviewer uses this probing style to determine how you have performed in the past. These questions often start out with "Give me an example," or "Tell me about a time," or "Describe a situation." They seek details of your past abilities and performance. Then the interviewer rates each response to determine and predict your future performance with her company. These situational questions are thought-provoking ones. The interviewer will likely take notes on each answer and continue the line of questioning, looking for *specifics*: specific details, specific illustrations. Practice answering these types of questions by giving concise, detailed examples. Be sure you select examples that clearly sell those skills in the 5 Point Agenda that you have shaped to meet this employer's needs. Be concise; tell the whole story in 60 seconds or less. You're unlikely to know in advance who will use this format, so be prepared. Typically, large organizations, human resources personnel, and recruiters are the ones to use this style. More and more college students are being asked these questions, but so are managers, senior executives, professionals, staff, and everyone else in between. Sandra, a senior human resources manager at a Fortune 500 company, explained it this way: "We are so worried about lawsuits, we now instruct our managers and HR people to ask only work-related questions that ask for specific examples. Every interviewee gets the same questions, designed to evaluate their skills to perform that specific job based on the examples they give us."

Some of the following questions are tagged with the word *situational* to tip you off that you need to offer concrete work examples. I've included several questions you might encounter, with appropriate responses. I advise you to prepare several examples in advance to help you sail through these challenging interviews.

Answering the Questions

Review the explanations and answers below, then choose your own words and formulate your answers to potential questions. The result: you'll be prepared to handle any question concisely, getting your point across in 60 seconds or less.

Personal: About You

1. *"Tell me about yourself."*
Too many candidates give their autobiography and waste this chance to capture and focus the interviewer's attention on

their ability to do the job. The best answer, which is also the most effective, is the 60 Second Sell.

2.   *"Why did you leave your last job?"*

I guarantee that you'll get asked this question, so having an appropriate, acceptable answer is a must. Good reasons to depart include wanting more challenge or growth opportunities, relocation, layoffs, or reorganization or downsizing that affected your duties. A typical answer might be, "The company went through a downsizing; that's why I'm available." Another answer might be, "My current employer is small and I've gone as far as I can with their organization. I'm looking for a challenge that will really use my abilities and strengths so I can continue to grow and make a contribution." A different response could be, "We've just relocated to this area to be near our family, and that's why I'm available."

3.   *"What is your greatest weakness?"*

I was teaching a recent job search seminar when an engineer blurted out loudly, "That is a really stupid question." Regardless, many employers learn a lot by asking this question. I always tell managers attending my seminar on hiring to ask this question because many times the job candidate gives them evidence of how they *cannot* do the job. Recently at a seminar with senior executives, a CFO related this story: "I was hiring for a staff accountant position. When I asked the guy to tell me his weaknesses he said, 'Well, sometimes I get the 3 and the 8 mixed up, but it all seems to come out okay in the end.' The 3 and the 8—we are in finance!" he exclaimed, emphasizing his exasperation with this confession. I repeat this example because this question causes many people to make a serious error and bare their souls or "come clean," as this applicant did.

If you think about this in advance and you have a written-out answer, it's really not that tough a question. I recommend that you pick something that has nothing to do with your ability to accomplish the job. An answer that I always used was, "Chocolate—I have a definite weakness for chocolate!" Ha, ha, ha, joke, joke, joke. A little humor in the interview is definitely okay. And often we would move on to the next question. But if the interviewer came back and said, "No, now really, what is your greatest weakness?" I might say:

"Well, you know, I can be pretty type A when I'm working on a project. I just get so absorbed, I forget to look at the time. Before I know it, the time to leave has long gone by and I'm still there. I guess that's a weakness. I guess I should realize that you should be able to leave right at five. But when I'm working on a project and I'm being creative, and things are rolling, I just stay on until I can get it done." Here a weakness or fault has been turned into a positive, appealing trait. Try to choose something that's not going to hurt your chances of getting hired. A better answer for our accountant might have been to say, "I have excellent computer user skills. I know Excel inside and out, but I am pretty weak at actual programming and would need more training if I were needed to write code for your software programs." No one's asking him to create enhanced software, and his answer actually reinforces his major selling point—his computer skills.

Another approach to this question is to discuss a skill you were weak in and then add how you'd taken a class and worked on mastering this skill and now it's something you do quite well.

With advance thought you can choose something similar that will have no negative impact on the hiring decision. Other acceptable responses include admitting you are a workaholic, that you are a perfectionist, or that you get impatient with your own performance and sometimes are too hard on yourself if you make a mistake.

4.   "What are your strengths?"

Respond with your 60 Second Sell. Tailor it to the particular needs of this job.

5.   "Tell me about your proudest accomplishment at your current (or last) employer." (Situational)

Review your 60 Second Sell and 5 Point Agenda. Think about what you're trying to stress, and then write down three big work-related accomplishments that demonstrate your ability to do the employer's job. Employment, community, or association work can often be examined to find just the right example to make your point. Avoid noting personal achievements such as "I lost seventy-five pounds" or "I won the 5K race." Better to illustrate with work accomplishments, citing specific examples such as, "I am proud of the donors and friends newsletter I started as a part of our fund-raising efforts. It has helped increase donations by 20%, and we've had a great deal of positive feedback on it."

6.   "You have a lot of experience. Why would you want this lower-level job?"

The employer fears you are overqualified and will get bored and want to leave the job quickly if he hires you. Or he may suspect that you are simply burned-out and looking for an easy job now and won't be productive. You have anticipated this question. Do not oversell your abilities. Do not show that you are desperate, that you'll take *any* job—that is always a major turnoff. Stress why this job fits for you now. Talk about life changes, need for more structure, desire to make a long-term contribution. You can say that you wish to spend more time with your family and therefore want a job with less travel or overtime demands. Be careful not to say you want an easy, no-stress job, causing the employer to doubt whether you would do all the work that needs to be done. One other mistake to avoid is saying, "I'm willing to start anywhere." You may mean it at that moment, but the employer worries that you'll be looking to get her job tomorrow, or at least expect a large salary raise quickly once you "prove yourself." It's sometimes wiser to search for a job that is a better fit if indeed this job level is way beneath your ability.

7. *"Describe how you work under tight pressure deadlines and give an example." (Situational)*

The interviewer is interested in your time-management skills, workload organization, and how you effectively deal with stress. Try: "In my current job, I try to plan out all major projects in a reverse timeline. I start with the deadline and work backward to set divisional deadlines for each part of the project. I work well under pressure. I have always made deadlines in the past. I use time-management and planning grids, to-do lists, project scheduling, and spreadsheets. I even plan for the inevitable snag or two that may come up. These tools help me to best utilize my time and to avoid becoming frantic and overloaded as the last hours of a deadline draw near. Additionally, I use email to be sure everyone on the team works together and is well aware of when and what is needed. By collaborating, everyone's stress level goes down."

8. *"What two or three things are most important to you in your job?"*

Select two or three points from your 5 Point Agenda and frame your answer to say, "It's important that I use my skills to be a productive contributor to my company. I believe when I'm using organizational and planning skills, I'm working at my best. That's important to me." Be sure to select two or three items that are essential to doing the employer's job successfully.

9. *"This is a very high-pressure job. Do you think you're up to it?"*

The only way to prove you can handle pressure is to give an example. Applicants for sales, customer service, operations, and top management positions often get this question. Create an example like this: "Cabinet sales is a high-pressure business. Our margins are tight and we constantly need new business. Last year we opened a new territory, and the heat was on for us to produce. I met with my sales team and we established new goals. I let them pick the reward structure that motivated them. Most chose a paid vacation, not higher commissions. So every week I sent a note with a picture of their goal—Hawaiian scenes, a freshly painted house, dollar bills—to keep up the momentum. It worked, and the entire department was rewarded for surpassing corporate's goals."

10. *"Why do you want to leave your present job?"*

Expect this question, as almost all employers ask it. Companies want to hear that you seek more challenge, more advancement, a promotion, more financial reward. You can also leave to shorten your commute, reduce the travel requirements in your job, or because your company is unstable. Try: "I have learned so much working for my current company, but there are no promotional opportunities. I enjoy challenges and learning new skills as well as improving my old ones. Therefore, I am seeking a new position at this time." Or: "I noticed that your company had an opening. I've been very happy at my present position, but the option to move to a good company, such as yours, and only have a ten-minute commute is very appealing. Right now I commute forty-five minutes to an hour each way." Or, for a small company, try, "I've gained a lot of experience at my other positions. But now I want an opportunity for more responsibility, to have greater impact on the end results. Your company will really allow me to see the fruits of my labor, and that is important to me."

11. *"Do you mind routine work?"*

The key here is to recognize that routine work is the job. Your answer should be, "I enjoy structure; it allows me to be efficient in doing the tasks correctly."

12. *"What motivates you?"*

"Using my strengths and abilities to be a highly productive employee. I take pride in my work and thrive when I use my skills." Fill in the blanks, naming the skills in your 5 Point Agenda.

13. *"How creative a problem solver are you?"*

This question is very tricky in that you aren't sure what the employer is getting at. You also want to know if there are big problems and not enough funds and resources available to fix them. Therefore, I recommend you answer with a question, to clarify what's being asked. Try: "In the past, I've been a resourceful problem solver. Could you be more specific about the types of problems I'll need to solve here? Then I can give you examples of what I've done in the past." Be sure to get a good answer at some point in the hiring process about the company's stability and the depth of the problems the company and your department face.

14. *"Describe your ideal job."*

Explain that the perfect job is one that uses your talents and allows you to be most productive. Mention several of the strengths from your 5 Point Agenda. The tendency for most job hunters is to get into elaborate discussions here about what they want—salary, benefits, work environment—and not focus on doing the employer's job. Save the salary and benefits discussions until after he makes the offer. For now, you still need to convince him you're the right one for the job. This is a great opportunity to stress that you enjoy learning new things, are adaptable, and are willing to take on new tasks as needed. Reiterating that you possess the traits of the ideal worker persona is always a plus.

15. *"What's the most difficult challenge you've faced in your life?" (Situational)*

You will need to discuss a specific example that demonstrates how tough the situation was and how you handled it. I recommend sticking to work-related situations. Personal tragedies, broken relationships, and sick family members are usually our most difficult challenges in life, but discussing them in an interview can be distracting or cause extreme emotional reactions within you. This could create a problem for you in handling the rest of the interview or raise doubts with the employer about your emotional stability and dependability on the job. It's best to stay away from these personal subjects. Avoid discussing coworker problems unless you can show how you changed your approach or attitude to improve the working relationship. If you have ever had to fire someone, then use that experience. Everyone finds it difficult to take away a person's livelihood. State how you tried to improve the worker's performance, carefully considered the decision, and then, with professionalism, terminated the employee.

16. *"What are you doing now to improve yourself?"*

Employers value employees who believe in lifelong learning. It is best to note that you are taking a course, using a tutorial, attending professional conferences or regular meetings, or reading a book to gain or improve a skill. You could say, "I am enrolled in the project manager certificate program and I'm working on earning that," or, "I am currently going to college at night to pursue a degree in business." Another option is to say, "I enjoy doing research on the Internet and spend free time downloading business articles we can use here to improve our division's website content."

17. *"What was the last book you read?"*

Often this is a question to see what you read off the job. A common mistake is to select a current hot business book and drop that title to look smart. More often than not, the next question will lead to an extensive discussion of that book's principles and theories and a defense of your opinions. So don't try to fake it to impress the interviewer—state a book you know well enough that you can talk about the plot or content. This isn't a critical question, so don't get too concerned if you answer with a novel and not a job or business book. One caution: be careful not to say that your life is so frenzied with kids at home that you never read. Instead say, "I enjoy reading magazines. I like *People*, and *Cooking Light* (or *Men's Health*, or *Sports Illustrated*)," noting a couple you regularly read.

18. *"Tell us about a personal goal that you still want to achieve."*

Share a goal that would increase your value as a worker. Cite a new skill—supervisor training, hiring experience, mastering a new software program—that, once learned, increases your value to the employer. Specialized degrees or training courses you want to complete can also be good choices.

19. *"Do you consider yourself successful?"*

Of course you do. So answer, "Yes, I do, and I bring a success attitude to work daily. I focus on being productive and contributing value to my organization." If you have had strong, positive performance reviews you could offer a copy of one and/or say: "I always give 110% to my job, doing the very best I can each day. In fact, in my last performance review I received top marks." This is likely to be verified, so don't exaggerate. A good performance review holds a great deal of weight—if you have one, use it. It's most persuasive to leave a copy with the interviewer.

20. *"What makes you qualified?"*

Using your 60 Second Sell will serve you best in responding to this one. It clearly reiterates the top reasons why you can perform in the job.

21. *"How do you handle stress?"*

Most jobs have some stress or pressure involved, and this question asks how you would respond to that stress. Be forewarned that if you bring up a specific stressful situation at work you will be asked all the details of why it happened, who contributed, and what you did and didn't do; also, you might possibly raise doubts about your effectiveness in handling the work without creating stressful environments for yourself and others. Be sure to prepare for this question in advance to prevent getting into hot water with a poor example. A good response could be: "Often stress results from inadequate time management and then feeling panicked at the end to get the job done and meet a deadline. I try to plan ahead and work efficiently to avoid last-minute pressure-cooker situations. There are times, though, when unforeseen circumstances create a stressful situation. Whenever that happens to me, I draw on my previous experience to help me decide how to effectively handle the present situation. I pride myself on being a very resourceful problem solver. The fact that I exercise three or four times a week also helps. I find it reduces my stress and increases my energy and ability to think clearly and to perform better at my job."

22. *"What do you do to support your professional development?"*

One Fortune 500 company asks every single interviewed applicant this question. Why? They want forward thinkers and good problem solvers, and they know that by hiring people who are continually learning they'll get those traits. Explain that you read trade journals, get industry e-newsletters, take classes, read books, or maintain membership in professional associations to remain current and advance your skills. If you are enrolled in college, specialty training, or a graduate program, then that is the answer for you.

Work/Job Experience

23. **"I'm not sure you are the right person for the job."**
Don't be put off by this question. Many employers have doubts about a candidate, though some never express them. See this for what it is—a terrific opportunity to sell yourself. Use the 60 Second Sell to respond. Sometimes it becomes apparent during the interview that you may not be a good fit for that particular job. My clients have had this happen, but nevertheless they did their best to sell their skill set. In several instances they were called back in a few weeks to interview for a higher-level (and better-paying) job, so market yourself appropriately.

24. **"Describe the worst supervisor you've ever had."**
    (Situational)
As much as you want to criticize an old boss and point out that person's faults, I suggest you reconsider. Many employers have told me this will reflect negatively on you if you do. Instead try this: "One boss didn't give me very much feedback. In fact, I only heard from him when there was a problem. Months might go by without any kind of feedback or idea of what he was thinking. Although I don't like to have someone standing over my shoulder, I do like feeling like part of a team, to have input, to exchange ideas, and get a feel that my work is in line with my boss's and the company's goals. Open communication, I guess, is what was lacking. I think that's really important to have between me and a supervisor." This answer demonstrates a positive response concerning the importance of teamwork in achieving the employer's goals.

In some positions, though, workers need to take on a great deal of autonomy. This is a growing trend. In such a case, you might frame your answer this way: "I'm good at my job and for two years I had a boss who gave me a great deal of autonomy. I flourished, meeting all the goals and at times exceeding them. My boss moved on, and the current supervisor is a micromanager. This is harder for me and most of the other employees to adjust to. I think having clear goals and then allowing me to proceed on my own is how I'm most productive."

25. *"What features of your previous job did you like?"* *(Situational)*

When you talk about things that you like, relate them to the job you're going to do for this potential employer. Talk specifically about things that she's going to have you do in this job, such as facilitate training sessions, create Excel spreadsheets, handle the budget, or organize a project from start to finish. Don't talk about perks such as "I loved the free pizza on Fridays."

26. *"What parts of your last job did you dislike?"* *(Situational)*

This is a tricky one. Be sure you point out something that won't affect your ability to do this employer's job. When you select an example, use information you know about the new job, such as the fact that all this company's publications are outsourced. At your old job, everything was done in-house. So you might answer with, "One of the things I really disliked was the length of time needed to complete printing projects. We did things in-house; many times everything was backed up several weeks. I found it frustrating to need seven weeks to complete a project that we could have turned around at a commercial printer within five days. I felt the process was not very productive or efficient."

27. *"Describe your ideal supervisor."*

This is really saying, "Can you work with me?" Frame your answer accordingly. Point out the type of management style that allows you to be the most productive on the job. Give an example of what the boss did such as, "she gave autonomy," or "we all felt we were an important part of the team, offering ideas and suggestions for improvements."

28. *"Describe a time when you were criticized for poor performance." (Situational)*

This question is a minefield. You must use a specific incident, yet carefully choose an example that demonstrates what you did to correct the situation. Select an example such as inadequate budgeting skills, which allows you to go on to say that you enrolled in a class and after several months you are now quite proficient. This demonstrates your ability to take constructive criticism and to improve. Avoid answers that deal with late arrivals, absenteeism, or interpersonal conflicts since these read as red flags, warning employers about your dependability and ability to fit into an organization.

29. *"I have several good people to choose from. Why should I hire you?"*

Most people are quite intimidated by this question, according to a recent HR survey. Don't be. Here's your chance to land the job. To convince the interviewer, say, "Listening to what you had to say about this job, I know you want someone like me who has the right skill set and a positive, 'get it done' attitude. I have . . . ," and then continue with your 60 Second Sell.

30. *"I'm a little worried about your lack of . . ."*

First, be sure you truly lack the skill or work experience. One client had loads of managerial experience working for a charity, but since it was unpaid, she mistakenly said she had no supervisory experience. Likewise, another career-counseling client had been teaching at the community college level for only one year. The faculty job required three years minimum. While we rehearsed questions for the interview, I interjected to inquire, "Don't you teach workshops in the job you have now?" Her answer was yes, she had done it for several years. Unfortunately for her, she interpreted teaching experience to mean *only* college teaching. Once she adjusted her answer to include her adult workshop training, she had many years of experience. Therefore, fully investigate your past work—paid and unpaid—and see if you don't have some additional experience for the job you want. Here's how our educator answered the question: "You are correct that I have only one year of college-level teaching, but I have conducted hundreds of workshops and seminars for adult learners for over seven years, and I've also given public lectures on this subject." Then go on and give more details showing that you do indeed have the necessary skill. In her case, she handed around some brochures that listed her as the teacher.

If you do indeed lack the stated experience, as is often the case with some specialized software, offer proof that you will learn quickly. You could say: "I download data from the mainframe using our proprietary software and produce the managers' reports. This involves extensive integration using both Word and Excel. I have a natural aptitude for using software, and I learn new applications very quickly. I mastered ours in a few weeks with no prior experience. Additionally, I would be willing to spend lunch hours and some evenings on my own time learning your software so I can come up to speed quickly."

The interviewer is concerned about a skill you lack, but when you show that you are eager to learn, it is impressive and influential. Another answer to try is: "I appreciate your honesty. I have excellent customer-service skills, but you are right, I have not been a salesperson. I know the keys to success are building good client relationships, persistence, using good time-management skills, being good at follow-up, and learning the trade. I have read numerous books on selling and understand the process. I intend to take seminars at my own expense to learn everything I can about selling. I am a hard worker who lets rejection roll off my back, and I know a lot about your products already. My goals include landing a sales job and then becoming one of the top salespeople in my company, based on my relationship-building skills and world-class customer service. I am determined to succeed."

31. *"Describe a difficult coworker you had to work with." (Situational)*

This one can be a dangerous minefield, so it's definitely not time for true confessions or to mention the screaming match you had with a jerk. Instead, think through your reply thoroughly before the interview. Craft an answer that shows the person was a poor performer. Commenting on attendance issues is a safe area, and your answer might sound like this: "In the finance department I compile all the general ledgers for our monthly accounting statements. I had a coworker who was supposed to do a major part of this job—getting all the financial records transferred and putting the data in a special order from all the business units. The problem was, this coworker overused the company's flex policy. She was often either out sick, having an outside meeting, or tending to her kids. I had to do ten hours of extra work in order to get the reports to our senior management by deadline. I complained to her to no avail, and eventually brought it to my boss's attention. Nothing happened. Later, when I was at a conference for three days, the coworker had to do all the general ledgers herself and didn't know I would be gone on the due date. The deadline came and went, and she never realized I hadn't bailed her out. Upon my return, my boss was in hot water with his boss. We had a meeting, and the coworker got reassigned. I got a promotion and small raise, and it turned out okay since getting the work done on time was priority one." Another way to approach this problem is to show off your problem solving skills. You could say, "I led the group's weekly meeting at 8:00 a.m. sharp and one employee always came in late. I mentioned how important it was that everyone show up on time but she didn't get the hint. After the third week of showing up late, I privately asked her why she wasn't able to make it promptly. She said she was responsible to drop her kids off at day care, but they didn't open until 7:30 a.m. With morning traffic plus time to park she just could not get to the meeting before 8:15. I resolved the issue and changed the meeting to 8:30, eliminating the problem.

32. *"Why have you changed jobs so frequently?"*

Job-hopping has become more common as we have become a more mobile society, particularly with all the downsizing and failed businesses. Dual-career families often relocate, with one spouse's job history showing numerous changes. Job-hopping is also a red-flag issue, something that really concerns an employer, especially when it takes months to learn the job. She worries that you'll just be trained, and then take off. Often the truth works best. If you have moved a lot, try, "My husband's position required us to move quite often. His last promotion guaranteed that we would remain in the area permanently so our son can attend all four years of high school here. I'm eager to get my career on track and bring long-term contributions to my employer. In my various jobs, I have developed excellent program-management skills; I know numerous software programs and quickly become a productive worker."

Or if the job changes came from obtaining better positions: "Each position allowed me to learn new skills, and every job was on a promotional path. Most have been with very small companies, where leaving was the only option for advancement. I'm now looking for a larger (or growing) organization where I can stay and make a long-term contribution."

33. *"Tell me about one of your failures at work."*
   (Situational)

This is a very tricky question. I suggest you answer by giving an example of a setback or a learning experience and show what you did to improve. "I decided that our company would benefit by having a lunchtime brown-bag training program. I lined up some speakers, scheduled the room, and sent out a notice. Four people showed out of more than eight hundred. The next event drew three people. I had failed, but I couldn't understand why. I asked numerous employees, and kept hearing that the topics *were* of interest. Most wanted to know what they'd learn and wanted a relaxed, fun setting. I asked a friend in marketing, who suggested using a snappy title for the program and each seminar. Changing the copy and using graphics did the trick. During a recent company survey, the luncheon program was rated as an important benefit and drew seventy-five to eighty employees per meeting. You see, looking at the failure to find a better solution was all that was needed." This answer shows you believe there aren't failures, only learning experiences, which is what is demonstrated here.

34. *"You have too much experience for this job. I have*
   some concerns about that."

Employers are reluctant to hire a person who is overqualified because they think he is unlikely to be happy or stay long or be seriously interested in doing the job. They do not want someone who is burned-out and sees their job as an easy paycheck. Often, you can be threatening to the interviewer, espe-

cially if you are truly suited for the interviewer's job. Examine
why you want the position. "I need a job" is not a response that
will endear you to an interviewer. You must have a logical, believable reason why a demotion is a good option. Try something like this: "My current position as controller requires ten
nights of travel per month. This has become an increasingly
difficult sacrifice for my family. I have decided to seek an accounting position that allows me to focus on my strengths—
taxes and audits—but that allows me to go home each evening.
The holding company I work for is typical of similar companies
in our industry—the controller position requires a lot of out-
of-town travel, which I no longer want to do. I believe the extensive financial skills I would bring would benefit your
organization in a positive way. I see this as a win-win situation
for both of us." Create a reasonable explanation. Showing desperation or willingness to take any job often makes the interviewer disqualify you. The company needs that job done and
you must show not only that you can do it but also that you *want*
to do it.

35. *"What was it about your last job that bothered you the most?" (Situational)*

Here the interviewer is looking for incompatibles: things
you dislike that are aspects of his company's job. The best way
to answer this is to select something that either is neutral or
would be a benefit. For example: "At my old company we had
slow computers, and the MS Office program was two versions
old. It took a lot of extra time and had fewer capabilities than
the new program. I found it bothersome, but my old company
didn't have the funds to update their equipment. As the editor
of my association's newsletter, I used top-of-the-line equipment
like you have here, and it made for a higher-quality, faster-
produced product. I'd look forward to using your equipment
and being more productive because of it."

36. *"Social media is an important part of people's lives. Do you use Facebook, Twitter, or any other social media? How often?"*

Watch it—this is dangerous territory. The employer is looking to see how active you are with social media. They want to uncover those people who are unable to go one hour without checking in. Many employers have instituted rules against using your cell phone during work because too many employees were checking email or looking at social media sites instead of working. Other employers block popular social media sites on their corporate network.

There are, of course, some employers that want to know you are computer savvy. The best option is to say that you do have an account or profile on a site but only check in occasionally.

37. *"Describe a significant mistake you made at your last job." (Situational)*

Select an example that demonstrates a learning experience and shows how you corrected the mistake. You might try something like: "I was under a very tight deadline, and we had a large volume of work to get done. Before signing them, I only glanced at some important letters my assistant had prepared. Unfortunately, the meeting time and location were incorrect. It was embarrassing. To correct the error I emailed each person and explained I'd made an error. I smoothed it over, but my boss noticed and spoke to me about it. I sat down with my assistant and calmly discussed how we could prevent these errors in the future. Together we decided that we would read the information to each other and triple-check to verify dates, times, and locations. We decided to try to replan our work time so there would be less of a push at the last minute to catch the day's mail. I volunteered to bring the mail to the post office so we wouldn't have to rush to get everything done before our one o'clock pickup." Here you've stressed teamwork, gaining staff cooperation, and problem solving. To err is human, but it is the *solutions* that you employ to fix or eliminate errors that matter to an employer.

38. *"You've worked for yourself now for a while, so why do you want to work for our company?"*

The truth is that self-employment is hard work. It takes endless hours, excellent business operation knowledge, capital, marketing skills, and perseverance to survive. Four out of five small businesses fail. The employer doesn't want an employee who is burned-out and wants an easy paycheck. And life changes—a divorce, an ill spouse—often create the need for a steady income and company benefits. These are usually the real reasons. Think through the answer and then respond appropriately. "I really am at my best training employees. I get outstanding evaluations and work hard to create an effective learning environment. I found that as a consultant at least 40% of my time was spent on marketing and business development. I failed to make follow-up calls because I would rather rework and improve my curriculum. I found I disliked 'selling,' so I made a decision to join a company. The job I really want is to spend all my time training others. I enjoy working with clients to determine their needs and then offer them a good seminar or training session to help employees improve on the job. Your company's position allows me to use my strengths as a trainer and focus on just that—training." It's important to calm any fears the employer may have about how difficult you might be to manage. Showing you work well with others is also a key point to stress.

39. *"Give me an example of a time you had to deal with criticism from your boss." (Situational)*

No one likes to be criticized. The truth is, most of us get a little hurt, maybe angry, definitely defensive. To answer this question, it is best to point out an idea that was criticized, or work that you went on to correct and improve. Be careful—your answer can cause the interviewer to question your ability to do their job. You could give an example such as: "I remember a time in a previous job when I was a new, younger staffer in a meeting of all the store department managers. We discussed increasing the company's sales among our younger customers. My idea was to advertise in a certain magazine. I was heavily criticized by two other department heads. I kept cool and re-stated my reasons, which were clear to me but not to them. After the meeting, I wrote out the idea, investigated, and noted some of our own market research that supported my sugges-tion. I sent it along to the sales manager. Months passed, and a competitor used my idea as part of their advertising campaign, with good success. My boss and the sales manager both reeval-uated my input then, and I believe I gained more respect from the department heads for my creative ideas after that."

If you select an example about your work's needing im-provement, demonstrate the steps you took to correct the situ-ation. "I gave a presentation to our executive group. I was nervous and not prepared for all the questions they asked, nor was I very good at ad-libbing when my PowerPoint program crashed. My boss outlined these points to me later. His feed-back was hard to take at the time, but I followed up on his sug-gestions. I worked on my presentation style—I took a class and even had myself videotaped. I also learned more about Power-Point. My boss's feedback was important in helping me improve my job performance, and recently he commented on how pol-ished and professional I am as a public speaker."

40. *"Tell me about something your boss did that you disliked." (Situational)*

It's best not to criticize your boss, though noting something like, "He smoked in our office," if you are certain the interviewer does not, is okay. If not, say, "I never really view a work relationship in those terms. We have a job to do and we all work together to do it well." Another option is to make light of it, saying, "He brought in doughnuts a few times a month, and I disliked it since I was blowing my diet, but boy were those glazed ones good," while smiling at the same time.

41. *"Explain how you organize and plan for major projects." (Situational)*

Stress in-depth planning and tracking, plus your efficient time management. "Currently, I use timelines, to-do lists, responsibility charts, staff progress meetings, problem-solving sessions, goal setting, and a sophisticated project-manager software system." If you are in charge of communicating with all parties involved in the project, be sure to elaborate on that too.

42. *"Describe your typical workday." (Situational)*

Here the interviewer wants to know specifics to confirm that you have handled most of the job's responsibilities before. Be sure to cover the most important duties in your answer, emphasizing the points in your 5 Point Agenda. Offer to give more specific details if he'd like, but try not to overwhelm him with a verbose and lengthy reply.

43. *"Have you ever had any problems with poor attendance?" (Situational)*

If the answer is no, say, "No, I haven't." This can and will be easily verified by your references. Lately, people have been unreliable and asking for extra time off, so, for many small employers, attendance is a major hiring issue. If you have had a problem, try to analyze what the problem was and offer a solution. Typical day care issues could be covered by saying, "When I was at ABC, my salary was lower than average, which created difficulties in finding appropriate day care. I often missed work when my child was sick because I could not afford a private sitter. I discussed this problem with my boss and my friends. I then decided that the situation wasn't fair to anyone. I asked my boss for a raise based on the quality of my work, which was high and well regarded. He explained that the company had no budget for raises. I then decided to look for a new job. Since I've been at X Company, I've never missed a day. I have a good day care situation that will take a sick child. I learned a lot about resourcefulness and my value as a worker. I put 110% into my job, and I know my current boss will attest to my productivity levels and good attendance."

If illness was the reason, you might say, "Once I was dealing with a personal illness and was absent often over several weeks. It was completely resolved within three months, and I'm quite healthy now and my most recent attendance has been excellent." From this question, the employer just wants assurances that your reliability won't be a problem.

44. *"Have you ever been responsible for managing financial budgets or department expenses?" (Situational)*

If the answer is yes, be specific. "Yes, I oversee my department's budget and approve all purchase orders and expenses. My budget is $xxx annually (fill in the blank) and requires me to be resourceful and cautious in spending my department's funds." It is always good to add that you are cautious about spending the organization's money.

45. *"What are the three most important responsibilities in your present job?" (Situational)*

Simply discuss the three areas that will be the most important to that employer in performing her job. Select them from your 5 Point Agenda.

46. *"Give me an example of when it was necessary to reach a goal within a very short period of time and what you did to achieve it."* *(Situational)*

Select an example that demonstrates resourcefulness, adaptability, and pitching in wherever necessary. For example: "The marketing department needed some new promotional material, and we had two weeks to research it, design it, and write the new copy. This was a big project. Two days after we got the assignment, the sales department secured a huge presentation to our most sought-after client. They needed the brochure created and printed in five days. Top priority. As the director of the communications department, I had to satisfy both of these customers. I reorganized my schedule and the graphic designer's. We forwarded calls to voice mail and stayed late, and within two days produced the copy and design needed to get the sales job done. The sales department made the pitch and we landed a very big account as a result. I can't say it was the brochure that did it. I think it was the desire to win, to reach the goal, that inner motivation of being part of the team. We all collaborated and worked very hard to get the results we wanted."

47. *"What would you do with an individual who is very angry and complaining to you?"* *(Situational)*

Think about what you do when faced with an angry person. Most angry people want someone to *listen* to their rage and *solve* their complaint. Often, just listening helps. Appropriate referrals or action steps to solve the problem might work also. Screaming or foul language might require you to ask the person to calm down and to suggest that when he can more calmly explain the problem, you'll work on the solution. Your response to this question might be: "In the call center I manage, escalated complaints come to me. Very angry, screaming people require a time-out, a cooling-off period. I express this by telling them I can only listen if they are calm and want my help in finding a solution. I have found that listening often dissipates the anger. They want their problem fixed or solved. I know that dissatisfied customers often do a lot of damage, repeating their troubles to countless others. I do my best to find a workable solution that our organization can deal with and that will satisfy the customer."

48. *"Tell me about a time when your work performance was low." (Situational)*

Work performance is affected by serious problems or tragedies that happen out of the office. Equally so, morale is low when a work environment threatens layoffs and reeks of job insecurity. Avoid an answer such as, "I was going through a divorce and my work really suffered," because employers are not as sympathetic to long-term poor performance. Select instead an example that deals with a short-lived personal or work crisis, and show your efforts to deal with the issue. For example, "Everyone was surprised when we came to work one morning and found out the company was being acquired. At first we were assured that no jobs would be terminated, but within three months layoffs began to happen. As the HR manager, people were coming to me looking for answers, but I was in the dark as much as they were. I got pretty depressed, and my new boss wouldn't answer any questions I asked on this issue. I began to feel so anxious at work that I didn't want to go. Finally, I went to see the new boss, insisting that we needed to talk, even as he tried to weasel out of it. I told him my concerns about how layoffs were being handled, and said I wanted to improve communication channels. Together, we set up a meeting with the new corporate HR VP and stated our need to improve morale and share information on termination plans. They knew we wanted to make the merger transition smoother, and that meeting built new paths toward collaboration. My own work improved once I could handle employees honestly and with some knowledge." Here you showed initiative—the desire to make a bad situation better. You took appropriate action and your low performance was brief. For a personal crisis, show good judgment addressing both the company's needs and your own, but be careful not to bring up a painful, tearful situation. "One Monday I got a call that my son had been taken to the hospital. He'd had a heart attack. My workload was enormous and I had a major meeting to lead on Friday. Rescheduling was not an option since so many other managers were coming in for this tactical event. I couldn't concentrate nor could I abandon my department. I called my boss and explained what happened. He couldn't do it himself so I suggested my assistant run the meeting in my place. She was the one who had created the PowerPoint presentation. I coached her by phone as best I could over the next two days. My performance was below par those few days since I was preoccupied with my son's condition, and my assistant had to handle a lot. At the meeting I had her make an announcement telling everyone what had happened and explaining that she was filling in for me for the rest of the day. Any questions could be emailed and I'd respond as soon as I was able. Upon my return, I found several nice emails offering prayers and support for my son. I took the time to send each person a handwritten note of thanks. I sent a glowing letter to my boss about my assistant's initiative, even though her meeting management wasn't flawless. She also got a nice big bouquet of flowers from me, and I began to work more closely with her, to groom her for a potential promotion." This is a good example because you took responsibility to delegate your work, communicated the problem to those affected, and found an acceptable solution. You also showed appreciation of staff, which is impressive too.

49. "Describe a time when you dealt with a stressful work situation." (Situational)

"I remember a time when we were short staffed over several weeks. I had been working a lot of overtime and so had my staff.

One employee called in sick, and that same day we had to make a 5:00 p.m. deadline that it would not be possible to extend. I called in the three remaining staff and told them the situation. I asked them how we could finish on time. They offered good ideas, and I had lunch delivered and told everyone that if we finished today they could come in at noon tomorrow. It was high pressure when everyone was running on low energy, but we did it. I also went to my boss the next day to discuss how we might readjust the workload while we were minus two people." This answer demonstrates teamwork, extra effort, and good problem-solving skills.

50. *"Describe a time when you felt you made a poor decision." (Situational)*

This is a very tricky question. Try to select an example where your boss admitted to you that she made a mistake too. You might say: "A few years ago, I remember my boss asked me to do a presentation to our board of directors. I worked on the material and asked my boss to let me run through the whole thing before the meeting. The day before I was to do that, my boss got tied up, so I never got her input on my research and data. I was embarrassed at the meeting when my figures and marketing data were heavily questioned. I got intimidated and nervous and stumbled through the questions. I made a poor choice in not getting others' input when my boss was unable to assist me. She did apologize to me later and took some responsibility for not making time to help me before the meeting. I learned a valuable lesson about teamwork that day, one that has helped me become a better supervisor."

51. *"Describe the environment that motivates you to be most productive." (Situational)*

This question often has you reveal some important clues to your true work style. Try: "I find that I am most productive in an organization that expects me to do a good job, that uses my strengths, and that has the necessary resources to accomplish the goals. If you check with my references at my last job, you'll find that I am results oriented, a self-starter. I'm happy when there are substantial volumes of work to complete, and I can be counted on to get it done right and on time." You might then ask, "How much autonomy will I have in this job?" Then you can learn how the job might suit your needs. Be sure to comment on any specifics in the interviewer's replies.

52. *"From what you understand about this job, what would you find difficult to do?"*

The interviewer is looking for you to expound upon some area of personal weakness. Perhaps you've heard something that makes *you* wonder about your performance ability. In that case, ask a question such as, "I need to know more about how you use your process assessments in the job." Or, "First could you tell me more about how large your budget is and the resources and staff assigned to the project?" Quantify the employer's needs and situation, and then answer. When citing a potential problem, attribute it to needing a brief time to learn their systems or software, etc., then explain that you learn quickly and that whatever appears to be a problem will easily be solved.

If this job seems to be in line with your abilities, just start with, "I don't see any difficulties and feel I'll quickly adjust to your systems," and then continue with your 60 Second Sell.

53. *"What is the most frustrating thing in your current (or last) position?" (Situational)*

Again, the interviewer is looking for incompatibility with the company's job. Be sure to cite something that will not be a negative influence and hurt your chances of getting hired. For example, "I hate dealing with angry patients" is a poor answer for a nurse seeking a position in a doctor's office. A better response would be: "At my current office, our front-desk staff makes numerous errors in regard to scheduling patients and not delivering messages. I then get calls from frantic patients who are upset that I never returned their calls. I've suggested I get a voice mail extension to have calls transferred to me, and my doctor has agreed, but it's been three months and it hasn't happened. I believe in providing the highest quality of care possible and am glad to hear you have a good system in place here. I become frustrated if we don't try to offer patients the best quality of care, especially since the patients in our oncology department are often very sick."

54. *"What do you find most challenging in working with customers or clients?" (Situational)*

Interpersonal skills and adaptability are the key points the interviewer is questioning. You might say, "I enjoy working with others. I excel at satisfying customers and solving problems. For example, . . ." Then go on to discuss a specific aspect of a past job where you dealt with customers' issues. A retail store department manager once said, "I remember an incident a few weeks back, when a customer came in complaining that her new red satin pajamas had bled into her expensive sheets, which she had also brought in. I asked her about the cost of the sheets, and they were $250. I refunded her money for the pajamas and apologized about the sheets, giving her the name of our risk-management specialist. I told her we'd call her in twenty-four hours about the sheets and gave her my card. I called four hours later, after I tested other pajamas we were selling and found that they did rub off just as the customer had said. I pulled the items, and we immediately sent the customer a check for $250 with our apologies. This solved the problem, and pulling the product and notifying other stores eliminated a potential catastrophe for them also." This answer outlines the problem, the solution, and the results. Always strive to tell your stories this way.

55. *"Describe the kinds of people you enjoy working with."*

This is easy since you can describe the types you enjoy. Try to correlate your response to what you know about the company culture. High-tech and emerging companies tend to be full of driven, type-A personalities. Mention how you love being part of a driving team pushing to do its best to innovate and improve. For smaller companies and nonprofits, you might mention how you value being affiliated with their business or mission and how you get along well with others. In larger companies, mention how you enjoy collaborating with a team, since most work there involves groups. A safe answer is always that you enjoy working with other people who take pride in their work, who are honest and act with integrity.

56. *"Describe the kinds of people you find it difficult to work with."*

This one isn't hard at all. Try saying, "People who are slackers and constant complainers. I don't understand how they take no pride in their work and don't focus on doing a good job." Or you could try, "I don't want to work with people who are liars, cheaters, or who have serious integrity issues." Ethics and honesty have become important values employers look for, so this answer works especially well for managers and executives.

57. *"How would you adapt to a team member going on extensive leave and your having to step up into a more senior role?"*

Give an example of leadership, whether it's supervising roles you have had on a previous job, heading a group project, or directing a committee. You may have volunteer managerial or leadership experience you can bring into play here. Mention that you have ambition and initiative, and that you are a self-starter but of course would work hard to learn as much from the departing employee as possible. You'd also talk to team members so everyone was clear on your new role and would ask each person for input on working together while the boss was out on leave.

58. *"Tell me about a time when you observed a coworker doing something inappropriate and how you handled it."*

Ethics questions can be very tricky, because your answer needs to demonstrate your integrity. Typically, people are using company resources or property for personal use, or abusing expense accounts. Sexual harassment or discrimination activities should be brought to HR's attention, so it's best to stay with personal examples that demonstrate your loyalty to the company. Here's a great example: "My job was to authorize all the sales account reps' expenses and send them on to be paid. The company was looking for cost-cutting measures and asked us to more fully adhere to rules on entertainment and travel. Many of our reps complained that the new per diem rates to cover food and hotels were too low for the major cities. Since they had to pay the difference, many started to pad everything else to avoid out-of-pocket costs. I decided we needed to review and alter the policy instead of 'enforcing' something that didn't work. I made an appointment with the CFO, whom I had never met. I explained the problem and proposed three alternative solutions. He agreed to review the matter, and I was to poll the team and let him know what the majority wanted. Within two weeks we had adjusted our policy and offered significantly higher per diems in large, expensive metropolitan areas. I made it clear to all reps that this change would only stay in place if expense-account padding stopped. They were involved in find-

ing the solution and were vested in it, so they stopped the un-
ethical practice."

59. *"How do you self-evaluate your work?"*

Of course you work to the highest standards and are as productive as possible. Stress two or three of your top selling
points, such as your coaching ability and the successful teams
you have built that exceeded goals, or how you organized a new
tracking system to save time or money. Likewise, you could
point out an accomplishment or a result you achieved, such as
higher attendance at an event you planned or more traffic that
came to your organization's website due to your technical expertise.

60. *"Give me an example of how your communications skills are used on the job."* (Situational)

"I work as the executive assistant to the VP of sales, so I
speak to customers and sales reps continually. I've developed
excellent customer-service skills and always use them for problem solving, which is frequently needed when talking to people
on the phone or through email. Additionally, I generate dozens
of reports for my boss. He hands me a brief outline and I write
out the complete sentences and paragraphs. I use Word, Excel,
and PowerPoint on his behalf almost daily and do most of the
writing myself. If you ask my former boss, he'll substantiate
this." It's sometimes good to add this extra piece at the end to
legitimize your answer. Never do this unless you are certain
the boss *will* confirm the facts you have stated.

61. *"Give us an example of where and how you took initiative and what the results were."* (Situational)

One HR director at a Fortune 100 company told me she has
put forth an initiative that directs hiring managers to select and
hire people who have "potential" and have demonstrated initia-

tive in their past job history. These are the future leaders, the HR director stated, as they show that they will be able to take the lead and take on more responsibility. Too often they have an employee who is good at her job but never takes it to the next level without being told to do so.

If you are looking to excel in management and/or be promoted, you must show that you are a self-starter. Give a solid example of when you came up with an idea and took it upon yourself to do something that delivered a specific result and helped the company. Specifically, note where you saved money or time, or added to the bottom line.

About the Employer

62. *"What do you know about our company?"*

The temptation here is to spend an hour regurgitating all the market research you've done on the company. Better to sum it all up in what they need, like this: "That I could be a strong contributor. I know you need someone who can . . ." Then go into your 60 Second Sell.

63. *"May we check with your current employer?"*

This question often makes job hunters very nervous because their employer doesn't know they are looking for a job. To say no, try this: "My current employer is not aware I am looking for a new position, and contacting him could jeopardize the job I have. I have the names of three references you can call who are very familiar with my work." If you can show copies of excellent past-performance appraisals, do so, but only if they are very good.

In large companies, you may have someone who can be a reference besides your immediate boss, so try this approach: "My immediate boss is unaware that I am looking for a more challenging position, and I'd prefer he not be called. I do work with the controller daily as part of my duties, and you could contact her. I've put her name and number first on my reference list. The other two people have worked with me in the past in supervisory roles. I am sure they can answer any questions you have."

64. *"What do you think of your current or previous boss?"*

If you love your boss, this is an easy one. If you find your boss difficult to work with, be careful when phrasing your answer. Negative comments send up a red flag signaling a problem employee. Resist the urge to bad-mouth your boss. Try, "My boss has extensive experience in the field and I've learned a lot working under her," or, "My boss had an open-door policy and was very approachable. I found this to be an asset in our working relationship."

65. *"We work a lot of late nights here. Is that going to cause any trouble at home?"*

"I am able and willing to work whatever hours you need me to. I expected that evenings would be necessary in this position, as they were in my previous position." Your reliability and dependability are what the employer is trying to determine. If you have no children, or they are grown, you can mention that as a way to stress your ability to meet their needs.

66. *"You've been with the same company for so many years, how will you cope with a new one?"*

The interviewer is concerned that you'll be slow to adapt and change. Dispel that notion. "I have always been flexible and adaptable in taking on new tasks. I have shown initiative and I pride myself on being a constant learner. You'd benefit from my . . ." Use your 60 Second Sell to point out the experience you'd bring.

67. *"How do you think your present/last boss would describe you?" (Situational)*

Whether you and your boss like each other is not the issue. Simply fall back on your 5 Point Agenda to illustrate your skills and describe your work. Mention three or four points that your boss would note and that are also important to doing this employer's job. Give an example of some task or project you've been praised for. If you plan to use your boss as a reference, it makes a very strong statement if you end by saying, "My boss will be happy to verify this; feel free to call her."

Firings/Layoffs/Resignations/Work Gaps

68. *"Have you ever been asked to resign?"*

The answer to this question is no. You were either fired or laid off, or you chose to quit. You may have been presented with the option of leaving, but you still chose to leave. Too many lawsuits have been initiated over this issue. Your former employer would not likely admit to forcing you out. Therefore, say no.

69. *"Were you fired from your last job?"*

People who have been fired are very fearful that no one is going to hire them again. Actually, your fear and concern are much stronger than the employer's. I've helped hundreds of clients who lost their jobs, and many went on to find better positions than the job that got away. In most instances, one is fired due to personality clashes rather than incompetence, so a firing is not going to stop you from being hired again. That stated, if you believe it might be held against you, be prepared because the way you answer this question can create a lot of doubt in the interviewer's mind.

To prepare an answer, first analyze what happened. Many situations are really layoffs—whether it was one hundred people or just you. Companies change direction and drop employees frequently. If you can explain the termination as a layoff, do so.

If you were fired because of a personality conflict, recognize that almost 80% of firings are the result of interpersonal conflict on the job. Incompetent workers keep their jobs, but people in power struggles or with personality conflicts can lose theirs. So if this is the reason you were fired, then take pen and paper and write out some sample answers. Analyze what took place and why you were let go. Let's say you couldn't get along with your supervisor. You had differences of opinion, and because of that, the supervisor eventually made the decision to fire you. Here's how to answer this very difficult question: "About a year ago I got a new supervisor and the company started heading in a new direction. My duties changed and the company decided it needed different skills from those I had to offer or could learn quickly, and that's why I am available." Another approach might be: "One of the most important things that I've learned since I left my last job is the importance of having open communication. My boss was not a person who talked about goals, expectations, or even defining the workload's priority. Instead, he reacted when something went wrong. I'm the type of person who likes to get feedback so that I know if I'm doing a good job, if I'm meeting expectations, or if something's going haywire, so I can work on correcting it." Sometimes the circumstances are okay to admit to: "There was a problem with the budget process at my last job. I thought we had more time to retrieve the information than we did. The information from other business areas needed to be analyzed, and we had no power to get other departments to respond faster. I created a conflict with my boss by asking him to contact those departments to get the information sent to us faster and in a different form. My boss did not like to make waves, so I guess we felt differently about solving this problem. Unfortunately, the reports were continually late without this process change, which caused problems, and he decided to let me go. I've learned a lot since then, and I know that it's going to be very important in my new job to make sure I find a supervisor that has open communication, is responsive, and that I work well with. If you call my former employer, he will tell you I was a good worker, that I brought strong financial and accounting skills to the workplace, and that I worked well in a supervisory capacity with my other staff. These strengths were never in question." As you can see, this is an answer that is well thought out. The candidate planned how to answer the question. Point out where there was a problem and where there wasn't, so the potential employer gets a feeling that, yes, maybe you just got a bad break with that supervisor because of poor communication and weak leadership.

70. *"Why did you leave your last job?"*

In this day and age, with downsizing and corporate layoffs happening all over the place, you're likely to find yourself laid off once or twice. To respond you might say: "My company, like so many others, has restructured, and my position was eliminated during the reorganization," or, "My company decided to close its regional office and my entire department was let go." In either answer end with, "That's why I am presently available." Be careful in this answer that your voice and tone don't express anger or desperation. It is important that you don't appear to want just any job, but to be seeking the right opportunity. You may *feel* desperate, but practice not letting that feeling sneak into your tone. You need to make the employer believe you really want *this* job, not just *any* job.

71. *"I've noticed there was a period of time when you weren't employed. Tell me about it."*

Examine your reason for the work gap. The most frequent reasons are time between employment, a personal illness, a family illness, failed self-employment, maternity leave, or raising young children. What's important here is to construct your answer to show that whatever the situation was, it has been resolved, and that your performance, attendance, and motivation will all be top-notch now.

To explain an illness say, "I needed surgery and my recovery was lengthy, but now I'm fine and more than able to go back to work." To explain children or maternity and just returning, try, "I took time off to have a child (children). I have been able to secure excellent day care that will ensure that I'll be able to work every day and be a productive employee." Be willing to answer any follow-up questions that the employer might ask, such as: *What will you do when the child is sick? Occasionally we need this person to work overtime—will that be a problem? What are the hours that the day care is open? How have you prepared to handle the pressures of this position and the demands of a new family member?* The employer's concerns center around (1) How productive will you be? (2) Will your mind be on your work? (3) Will you be reliable? (4) What ways will your situation impact your ability to do the job—no overtime, changing hours, absenteeism, etc. Your most important goal is to learn whether or not this employer's situation will work for you. The employer expects you to show up on time and to complete your assigned workload. I hired an assistant who insisted that she'd never missed a day of work while she was pregnant or when she returned after her first child. Her reference verified this. Once hired, she immediately began to experience problems—child care for two children was very expensive, and she wanted to change hours to fit her day care schedule and reduce her costs. Unfortunately, this was at the expense of closing the office early so she could go home. She lasted only two months, and once she was let go, my boss vowed never to hire a mother with young kids again. Many employers have had a bad experience like this. Therefore, when you are returning to work after an absence, arrange day care that will look after mildly sick children (flus, colds) and establish a secondary system (family, friend, neighbor, spouse) that will care for the child if the care center doesn't. Be sure that you have plenty of leeway to drop off and pick up your children. That way, if you need to work a little overtime, you will be able to. Don't expect or ask employers to change the position's hours to fit your day care schedule. If you can't work the hours—e.g., 9:00 to 6:00—then drop out of consideration for that job. It is best to be honest. Predetermine your necessary take-home salary by subtracting taxes and child-care costs. This allows you to judge potential jobs more realistically.

When answering these tricky questions, demonstrate that you have thought through the situation and found good solutions, and reassure the interviewer about your reliability and on-the-job productivity. Also, an interviewer may not ask these child-care questions, but she is thinking about them. It's best to offer a good offense by explaining the specifics of how you'll be dependable and productive at their job.

72. "You've been unemployed for quite a while; why haven't you obtained a job before this?"

Most job hunters underestimate the length of time the job-search process requires, so they take extended vacations or re-group because they are too drained by the layoff or firing. It's important to note that the average job search can take up to six months or more. If you've been unemployed for more than one year, you need a very good reason. An appropriate response might be: "I did take some time to evaluate my career and focus the direction of my search. I took a few classes, to enhance my skills. I've been actively job hunting for several months now and am meeting with employers to find a position that will utilize my skills and allow me to be a contributing part of the company's team."

If the unemployment was due to a personal problem or illness, you could explain with: "A personal crisis arose in my family that required my time and energy. It was difficult emotionally and so I left my position because my focus could not be on my job. Now the situation is completely resolved. I am ready and eager to work. I feel that my previous strengths (mention two or three of your most marketable abilities) will assist me in again being an asset to my employer." Sometimes you can mention the incident—illness, relocating an elderly parent, accident—but use your judgment. Employers know people have a lot of drama when going through a divorce or the death of a loved one or child and their work performance significantly suffers. You'd be better off to avoid these two situations in your answer. No employer will believe you've completely recovered from the death of your spouse in four weeks. I believe it is best not to give many details; instead, try to move on quickly and avoid a lengthy discussion of any difficult personal issue.

73. *What have you been doing while you have been laid off?" (Situational)*

Most job hunters simply say, "I've been job hunting," or "It's a lousy job market," but that is not what the employer wants to hear. If you've been out of work for more than six months, one CEO said you'd better be able to fill us in on how you used some of that time productively. In these circumstances, it's best to discuss a new skill you've learned. For example, "I just completed Rosetta Stone's Spanish course and I am rather good at conversation." You can add that you've learned to read and write it . . . noting your level of competency and why you undertook learning Spanish. Great if you note it's to help you on your job since you encounter many Hispanic customers in your line of work. Another approach might be to discuss how you stayed sharp by volunteering at a charity or for your professional association and then explain what you accomplished or what duties you performed when volunteering.

Illegal Questions

It is against the law to discriminate against an individual because of age, religion, race, nationality, gender, or skin color. But that doesn't stop employers from asking illegal questions. I believe some employers, not really skilled or trained in the art of interviewing, don't recognize that these *are* illegal questions. Some are ignorant; some just have gotten away with it in the past. And then there are those who ask them anyway. In fact, a female attorney was recently asked numerous illegal questions inquiring about her age and how many children she had—both very illegal areas, but partners in the firms asked her anyway. She wrote to say, "Being a working mother means you get dumped on, but senior partners will not hire you if you do not answer these questions."

Job hunters often wonder, how do you answer those illegal questions? Illegal or not, these questions still get asked and handling them in an interview is often quite challenging. Before you answer, think about this important consideration—*do you want this job?* The response you make is really based on whether or not you want the position. You may make a principled stand and say, "That's an illegal question and I choose not to answer it," but in this lawyer's case she'd never be hired. You don't want to offend the interviewer. Confrontation might make him feel ignorant and embarrassed, if he indeed didn't know that it was an illegal question, and could disqualify you as a candidate. Job hunters often claim to feel that the employer is testing them, but most employers aren't intentionally trying to break the law. Employers who attend my seminars on the hiring interview state that they don't want to ask any illegal questions. Yet they admit that they are frustrated because there is some personal stuff that they really want to know about. My advice is, if you are asked something illegal and you really want the job, simply answer it. Let me give you a couple of examples on handling these tricky situations in the next few questions.

74. *"Are you pregnant, or do you have any plans to have children in the near future?"*

Many of my clients say they've been asked this question. Most confess they were astounded. An appropriate answer would be, "I have no plans to have children in the near future." Or try, "Oh no, I'm not pregnant!" Say it with a smile and drop the topic.

75. *"How old are you?"*

The employer thinks you are too young, thus inexperienced, not reliable, and require too much training, or too old, wondering if you have lost the drive and are only looking for a paycheck. One client in his early fifties said almost every interviewer asked him if he still had the "fire in his belly," as they were put off by his white, thinning hair. You haven't got much choice but to answer this question. In the older worker's case, he mentioned his strong track record, his ability to motivate his team members, and how well he handled clients. He commented that he had recently implemented a new process at his job that saved the company a significant amount of money. In other words, he showed that he's innovative, has creative ideas, and still has some drive left. Another client, age twenty-four, said, "I'm in my mid-twenties. I have solid planning and organizational skills, and I am a very quick learner and willing to do whatever is needed. My computer experience in Word and Excel is at the expert level, which allows me to be highly productive and complete complex reports quickly. I have no obligations at home, so I can work late if you need me to. Additionally, I have had very good attendance at my current job, which my employer will verify."

76. **"What does your husband think about your traveling so much?"**

Just answer the question with: "Travel has always been a requirement in the previous positions I've held. I expect it to be a part of this job and it has never been a problem." If you are not married, say, "I am not married and am free to travel as needed."

77. **"How many kids do you have, and what are their ages?"**

Most moms returning to work will get asked this question, but any working parent should expect it. Employers want reassurance that your top priority at work is work. Briefly state how you intend to be reliable. Expect that the employer will grill your references and even try to reach your current boss to verify this claim. If you have a perfect solution like this mother, keep it short: "I have three boys, ages eleven, nine, and six. We have hired a nanny for child care." Another option is, "I checked and there's day care across the street. They have openings, so it's perfect to ensure that I'll be here when needed. They also have a late pickup, and my mother can help out if my daughter, who's three, is ill."

78. **"We do credit checks here. Are you financially responsible for any dependents?"**

This approach is looking to learn about whether you have children, are a single parent, or have an elderly parent you are caring for. The employer is concerned about your reliability and ability to stay focused on the job. A concise answer if you do have children or parents you care for is to say, "Yes, though I have solid day care and backup care so that my attendance at my jobs has been excellent." Expect this fact to be checked out with your references. If you have no one at home you can use a bit of humor and say "Just my dog Duffy," offering a big smile as you say it.

79. *"What does your wife think about having to move all the way to Nebraska?"*

Careful, this employer really wants to see if you will truly move to Nebraska and what obstacles your family might impose. A recent survey in *USA Today* revealed that many employees are reluctant to relocate. Seventy-five percent cited the impact on their children as the top reason not to move. Additional concerns included disinterest in the new location, concern over a spouse/partner's job, and quality-of-life issues. Relocation costs are very expensive for a company to undertake. Thus, it is imperative that your answer dispel the aforementioned concerns. A good reply would be: "Relocating to advance my career is a part of our family goals. Both my wife and I like the Midwest and welcome the chance to move there."

80. *"Who's going to care for your kids while you're at work?"*

Employers worry usually because another employee caused problems due to family demands. Most employers want reassurance that you will be dependable and productive and will pitch in when needed. Be sure to have solid day care arrangements in place so you can squelch any concerns. I've rarely found a case where an employer isn't understanding when something tragic happens to one of your family members, once you've been with the company for a while. But when he's hiring you, he simply wants to be sure that you're going to show up. So reassure him that you are a loyal and dedicated employee, and remove any reservations he may have by answering: "I have a dependable person who cares for my children even if they are ill. She takes them to appointments and activities, and is flexible so I can work overtime when I am needed."

81. *"What have you been doing while you have been unemployed so long?"*

One man with a work gap felt he was discriminated against when he explained that he spent the time home with his kids. His son had gotten ill and required extensive home care and doctor visits, which was the primary reason he'd left his job. We thus worked on an honest but less-revealing response: "After we had our second child, my wife got a great promotion so we elected to not use day care, and I remained home for three years. Our two kids are in second grade and kindergarten. I have remained active in the professional association, which has kept me current in the field." This worked, and he was hired. This client did not disclose all the truth. We both felt that details hurt him in the interview, and so we used the abridged version above and got better results.

82. *"We have a flextime policy, but I wondered about what activities you are involved in with your children and family, such as coaching. Can you tell me about those?"*

The employer is concerned about outside obligations, so carefully but truthfully answer this question. In fact, executives, managers, and staff employees often are committed to coaching their son's or daughter's team. Employers see these as time-consuming commitments, particularly if you are leaving early a lot of afternoons or are spending too much work time organizing team stuff. Equally so, employers recognize that they keep talented people by allowing them to balance work and family. Demonstrate that you are careful to finish your work and that you are productive and won't cause a conflict or other issues with the job and your boss. For example, a VP at a Fortune 500 company had a very demanding job and handled the question like this: "Last year I coached my son's basketball team and we had two assistant coaches—anytime I was needed at work, they took over. I arranged to have practice on Monday evenings since we have our senior leadership meeting that day and I am unlikely to be traveling. I had one of the moms be our communication leader, which dramatically helps my time management. Neither my boss nor anyone else has ever complained that coaching had interfered with my duties." His answer showed he had made careful arrangements to ensure his coaching didn't interfere with work. His employer was fine with the commitment, and so was the new one who hired him.

83. *"What country are you from?"*

You'll need to answer this question by reassuring the employer that she can legally employ you. Your answer might sound like this: "China. I have been in the United States for several years and have a valid green card and the proper working papers to be employed in this country. My experience includes . . ." Then reiterate your 60 Second Sell.

84. *"How well do you speak English?"*

This question needn't be discriminating. It could be used to determine placement. Many jobs require someone to be bilingual—fluent in two languages, like Spanish and English. The employer may also be asking to see what level your language skills are if you are an ESL worker. The employer may ask you to read something out loud in English—don't be embarrassed. They need to see if you can understand what you read and give directions from it.

Of course there are employers who hear an accent and may have some prejudice toward immigrants or anyone who speaks a bit differently. Try not to take offense. Instead, think before you respond, speak slowly, clearly, and explain how many years you have spoken the language. If you have a thick accent or are not yet proficient speaking English, comment that you are taking classes in both diction (speaking clearly) as well as English and grammar (speaking correctly) because you are always trying to improve yourself and your work performance.

85. *"The job requires you to work on Sunday. Will your religion cause a problem with that?"*

"Not at all." Nothing further need be said.

86. *"How will you adapt to this new job?"*

Just because the interviewer doesn't verbalize a discriminatory question doesn't mean he isn't thinking it. Here's an example that shows how a job hunter addressed the unspoken concern about his age and dispelled any preconceived ideas the interviewer might have held about older workers being inflexible or slow to pick up a new skill.

The candidate offered some reasonable proof that his age was an asset: "At my last job, I always proved to be very flexible and adaptable, frequently taking on new tasks and picking up new skills. I enjoy learning and teaching others. I have found that when I deal with difficult customers or solve complex problems I can draw upon my extensive experience, and this has repeatedly proved to be an asset in my former positions." You could then go on to describe a specific situation where your experience led you to make the right choice where a less experienced person might have made a mistake. Conclude that with age comes experience, and often the wisdom to make better decisions.

To summarize: If you are lucky, you may never be asked to answer an illegal question. If you get one, I suggest you answer the question quickly, and let the interview proceed.

Supervising Others

87. "Describe how you coach or mentor an employee, and give me a specific example." (Situational)

When asked about your work style, accuracy is your best option. Some delegate everything; some retain ownership and manage more tightly. There isn't a right or wrong answer, but in larger organizations there's an emphasis on team building. Collaboration—whether it's across groups or departments or in smaller teams—is the growing trend. Therefore, you are always safe retelling a story where you empowered an employee with additional training, or imparted some new insight for solving a problem, or worked together and pulled in other departments to get needed results. Employers like leaders who get results, and you need to show that this is something you have done and will continue to do.

88. "How would you influence someone to accept your ideas?"

The interviewer is interested in evaluating the depth of your communication skills and your ability to persuade others. Try: "I've learned that it is important to offer an idea using the right framework. It is important to look at the person or persons evaluating the idea and then determine the best approach that will appeal to them—maybe it's a chart with documented research, or a brief written report, or even a photo or illustration. Of course, I always have a rationale for why and how the idea will work. I try to think through the details beforehand. I'm open-minded, and I seek feedback to improve the idea, or implement it so it will work well." Another approach might be: "In sales the key is always to stress the benefits to the person I'm talking to. That's exactly the approach I use."

89. *"Tell me about an unpopular decision you had to make." (Situational)*

Positions of responsibility often require making hard choices. Select a time when you chose the lesser of two evils or when you provided solid explanations for a cost-cutting measure. You could say: "Our company was downsizing and we had to trim our labor costs. As the department manager, I selected dropping benefits and not terminating our employees. I sat down with the department's staff, stated the problem, and asked for their input. As a group, they all wanted to fire the most recently hired. Unfortunately, those new jobs were critical to the company's future. I decided to eliminate all insurance benefits (life, dental, disability, and retirement) but retain the medical coverage with a small co-payment. Many of our longer-term staff complained. I listened to them, but did what I felt served the company and department best."

If you ever had to fire a well-liked person, you might say: "I had a very popular employee work for me who was ineffective and had low performance in her job. She was very friendly but not able to learn the computer skills we needed. I elected to fire her. One person complained all the way up to the CEO. They admitted her work was inferior but said she was such a nice person that I should not have fired her. Although my boss agreed with my choice, I took the heat. Then I carefully hired a new person who had the necessary skills. I purposely hired someone who would blend in well with our other staff. In the end, it was the best thing for the department though rather difficult for me."

90. *"Describe a time when you reprimanded an employee for poor performance." (Situational)*

Show how you have given clear direction, coaching, and/or training to enable others to improve at their job. "I was assigned a new administrative assistant, and she repeatedly made mistakes typing correspondence for me. If she had carefully proofread the letters, she would surely have corrected the errors. I sat down with her and brought one letter noting all my corrections. I nicely told her that I was finding too many errors in the letters and asked if she proofed each letter before she gave it to me. She said no because she felt I wanted them quickly and I always seemed to make changes anyway. I told her that I expected her to proof each letter and make all corrections before she gave them to me. It was very important that our correspondence be perfect before we mailed it out. Since most of the work was highly technical, I suggested she take a class on proofreading and editing, which she did. As a result, her performance significantly improved."

91. *"Describe your management style in dealing with staff." (Situational)*

When you researched the company you may have gotten some insight into its managerial style. During the interview process they may offer information that gives clues into their culture. The more you know about the employer, the easier it will be to frame your answer to demonstrate your competent leadership capabilities. There are many management styles, but the most important aspect in evaluating leadership is results. Some managers use firm decision making, others micromanage to see that things get done. Some prefer an open, approachable style; some lack backbone; some don't even deserve their job. Dictatorial styles are very outdated, but some supervisors still act that way. Lately, bigger companies use teams, and coaching the team with solid goals and objectives while giving people autonomy and holding them accountable is becoming more popular.

Analyze your style and what you know about the company, then create your answer. An example might sound like this: "At my current job, it's important to be a firm credit manager who enforces the company's rules. I expect myself and my staff to do that. I hold each person accountable for doing their job and following company policies. I am also a reasonable person when negotiation is required to aid clients in the process of paying their bills. I listen to concerns or ideas from coworkers and staff. I'll review clients' needs and, based on the company's goals, will change policies that become outdated or ineffective. I work closely with sales to enable the company to grow without extensive or undue risk. In credit, we hear a lot of stories and I teach my staff that people lie and they must keep in mind that their job is to collect the money owed the company. Using professionalism and legal guidelines, we all work together and do just that." Another way to answer this is to offer some evidence, like past performance reviews or commendations for your management style. You might say: "Good question. In fact my current company has our staffers rate the managers. My current boss has rated me in his performance evaluation as a superior and effective leader. Here is a copy of the review. The report says I bring intelligent leadership to my position. I'm defined as energetic and enthusiastic and positive. They say I am articulate in defining the company's vision and goals. I recognize and reward my people as they strive to obtain results." A more humble person might let the report do the talking, saying, "Here's a performance review I received a few months back. As you can see, my boss rated my leadership skills as being quite strong." Then hand the interviewer the report and point to: "Karla is dynamic, brimming with enthusiasm, and extremely perceptive. Even more important, she gets results with people. She has a vision, sets clear goals, and brings out the best in people with her great sense of humor and excellent communication skills. She is one of the most capable and dedicated managers in this company." Leave a copy of that review with the interviewer.

92. *"How would you rate yourself as a leader? A supervisor? An employee?"*

Analytical individuals often rate themselves low because they look to improve everything, including themselves, but that is not a good approach here. Start with the employee part first. You could say, "I'm a highly regarded employee because I'm productive and good at what I do." As a supervisor and manager, continue to say: "I treat everyone fairly, and that allows me to have a good working relationship with my staff. I'm approachable and have an open-door policy, but I also hold each person accountable for doing his job well and achieving the department's goals. In the past, my department has always been recognized for its productivity under my leadership." You can say this even if you've won no awards. All departments have goals, and if you achieve yours then it signifies that you are in sync with the company's demands.

93. *"Give us an example of an unethical action you witnessed and what you did about it." (Situational)*

Several people have said this question stumped them. If you have a situation where you did the right thing and it turned out well, describe that. For example, "It became apparent to me that one of the people in our office was stealing. I would never accuse someone, but my assistant told me about this problem and so one night I had an IT specialist help me look at the employee's computer and hard drive. Indeed, he was embezzling a great deal of money. Due to the serious nature of this, I called our CFO at home and asked him to come back to work, outlining the situation. We stayed there for hours as we uncovered the necessary data to prove our case. The CFO had the person arrested and prosecuted. I hope I never have to deal with that again, but we handled the situation professionally and quickly to prevent further theft."

Another appropriate answer would be: "One of the men in

my department had a pretty strong sense of humor and he often emailed jokes to a bunch of the guys. They were funny and harmless, at least in the first month or so. Then he sent a joke that had some racial slurs. Next day, he sent another. He must have been being encouraged, because on the third day he started hitting on sexual themes. I don't supervise this guy, but I got concerned since my assistant often reads my email for me when I travel. So I went to him and said I thought it best if he sent only clean jokes, as an unintended recipient could see it. Apparently he took me off the list, but ragged on me in emails to the others. He used some ethnic slurs to describe me. I was told by my assistant, whose friend had seen them on her boss's email. This was bothering me and was just downright wrong, plus now it was distracting and taking time from the job. It was getting out of hand, so I told my boss and our VP of HR." Reporting this was appropriate and the interviewer would assume this person had used good judgment since no company wants sexual harassment or discrimination suits, and this kind of "fun" at work often leads to those problems.

94. *Give us a detailed example of how you handle a low performer.*

The key here is to show you are an effective leader. You may have a story where you can show how you coached and provided key direction to help a low performer improve. One client, a sales manager who oversaw seventeen account representatives, related a story he used in answering this question. He said: "Ours is a competitive industry, and it's easy to lose a customer if your account people aren't attentive and responsive to their needs. Last year, I had one lady, Annie, who was a lower-level player, but she went down to the bottom quickly one month. I went to her and asked what was going on and she confessed her husband had left her and was now living with his secretary. She was pretty emotional and it was obvious to me this was a devastating personal issue. I suggested she take family leave while she dealt with this challenging time. She refused. I also suggested she seek a counselor and sent her to HR. They also recommended the Family and Medical Leave Act to allow her to keep her job, but she felt she needed the income. Unfortunately she wasn't doing any work. A couple weeks later I got a call from one of her customers complaining that she hadn't responded to his emails on needing to make an order. I took care of the customer myself, and sent the customer a gift with a note saying how much we appreciated her business. I went to Annie and told her what happened. I gave her a verbal warning and also wrote up the incident, issuing a firm warning. I gave her thirty days to improve and stated that any more customer complaints would result in termination. Didn't take long before another customer emailed me saying he'd gone with a new vendor, dumping us due to her poor service. I had to terminate Annie after this happened. I spent some time with two of my lower producers who had smaller territories. I offered them both Annie's customers and said if they could service them and *please* them, I'd allow them to keep the clients. I spent time coaching them and did some field work with each. It paid off. We had a great year in sales, surpassing our quotas." They loved his answer and later told him it was the reason he secured this new job.

95. *What strategies have you used to address diversity challenges? What were the positives and the negatives?*

Having managers implement diversity initiatives is a big concern for many global employers. Addressing the need to promote tolerance, acceptance, and inclusion is the key to handling this management objective. Positives are that more input from every person on the team often allows you to come up with new ideas, productivity, and process/system or design improvements. Many customers are from different ethnic or cultural backgrounds, so being savvy on how to act and what to say shows insight and good business acumen. Negatives are that some people are resistant to changes and need additional training classes and coaching to be more sensitive on this issue.

Technical Expertise and Specialty Questions

A professor seeking a new college position should expect numerous questions on his subject area, any ongoing research, teaching style, etc. A nurse should know her area well and what common problems she might encounter and need to handle. Anyone in a specialty area should think about trends affecting their industry.

Engineers, programmers, IT managers, and other technical people should assume they will be asked very specific questions related to their field and area of expertise. Once you've gained experience in an industry and job area, you'll need to be able to give examples and answer related questions. These questions can be either very challenging or easy to answer, depending on the interviewer and their own expertise. If they start to probe your knowledge in an area you don't know well, be honest. No BS—you won't bluff your way through. Oftentimes they are trying to stump you or see how forthcoming you'll be.

A software engineer should expect numerous questions concerning coding, the languages she knows, and the types of software and applications she has worked on and her platform expertise. Expect to be probed outside your direct area of specialty and be ready to give your thoughts on current industry trends or notable changes. A popular question for technical people is to be asked to design an app and explain how others would use it. Another interviewer may say, "design something." A client who recently interviewed at Google spent the day there with five different interviews and had an informal lunch as part of his process. He got the offer and shared this insight about the interview process: "Prepare for technical questions, and to answer leadership-related questions as well." Google asked lots of situational and behavioral questions too. He had interviewed at other highly desirable companies and found them all to be challenging and asking both technical and numerous situational questions.

To prepare for a technical interview, create five to ten questions you think you might get asked concerning your field or particular specialty area. Then practice answering them. Again, remember the guidelines—short, concise answers of less than 60 seconds, using real work examples to demonstrate how you've successfully done this work before.

96. *"Tell me about your experience using Photoshop (or another specific software program)." (Situational)*

The question becomes much more difficult if the interviewer asks about a program you haven't used or have just barely tried. If you know the company is using different software, you might continue to say, for example: "At my current job, we use customized proprietary design software. I have had some experience with Photoshop itself several years ago. The software I currently use has many of the same design tools as Photoshop. I know all the concepts since I'm creating graphics almost daily and have mastered general design tools thoroughly. It would take only a short time to become proficient in it, and I could do it—it's even on my list of new software I planned to learn this year." Another approach might be to say: "I've not used that design software. The one I do know has many similar elements so it's a great foundation to build upon. I'd certainly be willing to use some of my own time for a class or tutorial to speed up the learning process." This may not be enough to get the job if the employer refuses to train someone. Showing your design work can make an impression and may be enough to snag the job, especially if no one else comes along with years of experience with that software, or he or she lacks the creative talent you have in other areas.

97. *"Explain in detail your daily computer experience and what software programs you use." (Situational)*

Begin by asking what they are using. Computer skills are essential in most people's jobs, and even executives now handle their own reports, email, and electronic calendars. The employer wants a clear picture of your true ability, and too many people have bluffed their way through the interview sounding like their computer skills were much more advanced than they are in real life. Since affirming your skill level is critical, you might say, "Do you use Microsoft Office?" If so, continue with: "I work mostly with three programs, Word, Outlook, and Excel. I'm a very advanced user of Word and I create reports daily. I also compose spreadsheets to track my department's budget expenses and monitor project timelines using Excel. In Outlook, I handle all my email and organize it for easy retrieval so I can find important files. I sync it to my phone, so I have my calendar with me at all times." This example shows a clear overview of your skills and confirms that you are an advanced user.

98. *"Describe your experience using a database in detail." (Situational)*

First, *ask* what database they use. Maybe it's Access, or MySQL, or even a proprietary program you would only know if you were an employee. If you do have experience and skill in this particular database, great—give specific details about your level of ability. If you don't have knowledge of this database, explain that since most databases operate on the same principles, and you've worked on them for years and had to learn a new one at your current job, you know you'd learn theirs equally fast. This question gives you a good opportunity to show what you can do. Hopefully, you remembered to bring a sample of some database reports you created or even brought your laptop to demonstrate how you use a database in your job.

99. "Do you know how to blog?"

Many people blog today. Some may be job related, but the vast majority of individuals are simply posting from personal interest. An employer is wondering about your creativity and communication skills. If you blog, be sure to bring along a couple of your more popular posts. Practice discussing why you're passionate about the subject, what inspires you, how often you post, and how many followers you have. You could add in what techniques you've learned to use to attract more followers, especially if blogging is related to the job.

100. "Name the one skill that you'll bring to this job that will make you successful."

The answer is to select the most important skill in your 5 Point Agenda and state that. Be sure you answer the question—the interviewer asked for one skill, so select and state just one. It shows you are a careful listener.

101. "How do you communicate with different types of people, for example analytical IT people versus sales people?"

The real concern is whether you can talk to anybody. If you can, be sure to offer a clear example of working effectively with both types. Offer a situation where you, a technical person, worked with someone who wasn't technical such as HR or a customer. Explain how you are able to simplify your descriptions and answers so that these nontechnical people understand. You can often offer to show a diagram or draw an illustration to help clarify your comments, which have been successful in communicating your points.

Questions for College Students and New Grads

It used to be that most new graduates had little or no related work experience when they interviewed for their first professional job. Today, a new grad can be anywhere from twenty-two to fifty years old, some having notable experience behind them. The average student earning an advanced college degree is now in his thirties, and quite a few are over forty. Sometimes, you may have a high GPA but are ineffective in marketing yourself and thus find landing the right job more difficult than you anticipated.

Preparation can help relieve some of the anxiety and allow you to effectively communicate the skills you do have. When you prepare for the interview, make sure your answers draw from both academic and work experience. Many new graduates have had only service jobs—working in a fast-food restaurant or retail store. Don't underestimate this experience! You still needed to show up and use teamwork and communication skills to keep the job. You also learned customer-service skills and how to work under pressure. For employers hiring new grads, dependability is a big concern, so use your previous jobs—whatever they were—to illustrate your reliability. Be sure to examine all work experience and activities for evidence of leadership or business skills, organizational abilities, time-management skills, research, analysis, teamwork, planning, and computer and writing abilities.

To prepare for the interview, talk to people who hold the job you want. Ask them about the skills most important to their job. Then develop your 5 Point Agenda and 60 Second Sell after you have researched and understood the necessary job duties and skills.

Practice answering questions with full and complete responses that get your point across in 60 seconds or less. Here are some questions you need to be able to effectively answer.

102. *"You have no real world experience with what this job requires. If presented with an assignment/ project with real world demands and deadlines, how will you meet these needs?"*

This is the time when you need to bring up specific school projects and assignments that dealt with problems in a similar way. The employer is questioning how you think and handle things. You might say, "I would take the whole assignment or project and work on it in smaller, more manageable portions. I would create a timeline for each part, which would allow me to complete the assignment within the required timeframe. I would also touch base frequently with my boss to ensure I was getting the work done correctly."

103. *"What led you to choose your field of study or major?"*

"Liberal arts has taught me to think out problems and research and analyze data. I've found sociology to be interesting with its broad-based analysis of society's behavior patterns. My classes required eight to nine books per course so I've developed excellent time-management skills for tackling a heavy workload. I am a great researcher as well as a good communicator with strong writing skills. I did term papers on numerous subjects all four years, which fine-tuned my ability to communicate effectively and clearly, and I learned to address the message to the appropriate audience." Another approach is to show how your major is reflective of your natural abilities and passion. If you were a business major, your answer might be very specific, such as: "I started out on the business track and took Fundamentals of Accounting my freshman year. I loved it. I loved the analytical challenge, and I've always had a strong ability when working with numbers. I decided to be an accountant after that class and am a student member of the state CPA society. It's a field I know I will succeed in, as I've done very well in my college program."

104. *"What are your long-range and short-range goals and objectives? How are you preparing yourself to achieve them?"*

The interviewer wants to see how focused you are, how realistic, or even if you have a clue about what you want to do. The interviewer wonders about the training time that you'll need to become productive and how long you'll stay once they have invested time training you. A good response might be a very honest one. "My short-term goal is to get a job that will provide me with the training and environment to use the skills I've developed in college. I'm a very hard worker and a quick learner, so I want an environment where I can contribute. I believe that once I'm working, I'll be exposed to many areas of business that I haven't seen yet, so I plan to keep my long-term options open while I explore numerous possibilities." This response doesn't jeopardize your chances for a position by mapping out a career agenda, such as "next year I'm off to law school," that doesn't fit into the employer's agenda. Showing flexibility, adaptability, and a realistic attitude about your future opportunities is the appropriate response.

105. *"Your grades seem mediocre at best. Why is that?"*

Do not get defensive. Organizations are full of people who did not graduate at the top of their class. Instead, discuss what areas you struggled in and what you learned. Mention an appealing strength too. You might say: "I think I learned the hard way and paid a price for spending too much time having fun and being popular. You'll notice my grades improved significantly after mid-junior year. My adviser and my father were both upset with my performance up to that point, and my dad withdrew his financial support. So I got a job and took out a loan to finish. Once I was paying for school, I put my entire effort into it. My grades improved. I now know the value of working hard, and I am proud I finished and didn't drop out. I do have some good skills I'd bring to the job. I excel in planning, and I have good time-management skills, having balanced a job and college." Accepting responsibility and showing you have learned from your mistakes makes a solid case to support your candidacy.

106. *"Describe your ideal job and its location."*

Tricky question, since you often don't know what your ideal job is and so you say you'll move anywhere. Most students do move to get a job. Analyze where you will and won't move. Then respond with: "I am willing to move wherever the company needs me, though I'm concentrating my search on the East Coast. My ideal job is in an environment that allows me to learn, gain new skills, and be a productive worker. It is also very important for me to know that I'm helping people through my efforts." Or end with, "It's important that I make a contribution to the company." You may add something that shows you're a little knowledgeable about the job. "Last summer I took an unpaid internship at the Lung Foundation. I worked on two fund-raising projects and their direct-mail campaign. This position gave me some insight into a career in fund-raising—a job I feel is important, meaningful, and one I want to do and do well."

107. *"If I were to ask your previous manager about what you need to improve, what would he or she say?"* (Situational)

This is a tough one because they want to know an area you're weak in, and what you're doing about the weakness. The key is to show you are improving. Stay away from anything related to attendance or reliability unless you have corrected it. One grad said: "I worked at the mall in Macy's two summers ago. A bunch of friends were going to the beach one day, so I called in sick and went with them. The boss found out and was really mad—he fired me. My dad was furious and took the car away. I learned my lesson. Since then I've worked at a pizza place on campus part-time, and I am always there. My boss will tell you I'm the one they call in to cover for others now. Here's his number on my reference sheet if you wish to call him."

108. *"You learned a lot of theory in school—how will you apply that knowledge on the job?"*

It's best to admit you'll need to learn as you go and hope to find a mentor to help. A short but effective answer could be: "You're right, and I know that in real life business practices aren't always what they're supposed to be. I expect to learn a great deal on the job and to expand my abilities. I also hope to find a mentor to help me adjust more quickly and show me what will and won't work." You might try giving an example of how you've witnessed theory and business practices differ. For example, "I did an internship last year at an accounting firm. A new grad had recently started when he took a call from a client's staff person concerning her vacation and overtime pay. He offered his own advice on whether the employee was due extra pay and overtime, which caused a big problem for the client's owner. In theory, the guy was right, but this client got very angry, yelled at one of the partners, and they even moved their account to another firm because the client was so upset this 'newbie' offered business advice and didn't think it would be first best to discuss it with the client directly, not the employee. I saw up front that poorly handled client relations have serious consequences and business-practice skills come from experience, not just school or book theory. I hope that working here I'd learn a lot from you."

109. *"Tell me specifically at what level you are comfortable using Excel (or Java, Photoshop, or PowerPoint, etc.). We expect you to demonstrate this ability."*

It seems that *every* grad says they have advanced or expert user skills, so many companies will ask you to quantify them. Be accurate, specific, and clear. Don't undersell or exaggerate. Define your skill level by painting a picture, such as: "I use Word daily. I write term papers, reports, and often insert the complex Excel charts I've created. Some reports were twenty-five to thirty pages. I worked in a secretarial pool last summer and all I did was handle the monthly budget Excel spreadsheets and report creation." Another choice: "In several of my classes we had to make sophisticated PowerPoint presentations. I've gotten really good at developing my own creative templates and design styles. I can create slides, of course, and outlines and do a top-notch PowerPoint presentation from conception to completion. I worked on many with more than one hundred slides. Some had to be concise but stress the message quickly—I've become good at communicating the message in the needed format and length."

110. *"How will you adapt to working Monday to Friday from eight to five?"*

This is an adjustment after the freedom of college. If you've held a part-time job then you can stress time-management skills developed balancing your hours working and being in school. You might say: "I never was one to be up late since I always had a 9:00 a.m. class. I needed to support myself in college, so I had classes followed by a part-time job, averaging at least nine-hour days during most weeks. I am eager now to be out of the classroom and working full-time to get my career going and to apply what I have learned. I think I'll adjust very easily."

111. *"What college subjects did you like best? Least? Why?"*

This tells the interviewer your strengths and weaknesses—and therein lies the tricky part. Your answer must illustrate interest in areas necessary to do the job and point only to unrelated subjects as ones you disliked. You could create an answer like this, substituting your favorite subject: "Psychology classes were my favorites as well as my major. I loved learning about human behavior and interactions, helping others to deal with behavioral difficulties and to understand themselves better. I least liked the modern art class. I found it too abstract for me. I enjoyed the Renaissance period much better."

112. *"Do you have plans for continued study and an advanced degree?"*

Tricky question here. The interviewer is trying another avenue to assess your goals and how they will fit into his organization's needs. If you don't have plans simply say, "At this time, I plan to land a position and work hard to be productive and learn as much as I can to excel in the field. I don't have any current plans to go on with my studies." If you are planning to do so, you could say: "I plan to get two or three years of experience doing engineering work first, and then I think I'd like to enroll in an evening MBA program. I know that it's very demanding to handle both, but I think I can because I worked all through college. Right now, I feel it is important to move from the classroom to a manufacturing setting because there's a lot to learn on the job before I pursue more education."

113. *"In what part-time or summer jobs have you been most interested? Be specific."* (Situational)

Most part-time jobs are not interesting and are often taken just for the money. Try to answer the question by noting something you did like: "I worked as a receptionist for a real estate office. I enjoyed talking to people who called, especially when I could answer their questions or solve their problems. The best part of my job was a small, two-week project I worked on. The secretary got sick so I stepped in and did a large spreadsheet project. My boss was thrilled that I knew Excel. I finished the project pretty quickly. I really enjoyed it and want a position that requires a lot of Excel work."

114. *"What bothered you most in your last part-time or summer job?" (Situational)*

This is a way to learn how well you work with others and how flexible and dependable you are. It's very unwise to talk negatively about the company or the former boss. So answer carefully, possibly saying, "Last summer I was working at a retail store, and we often had nothing to do when there were slow times without customers. I hated standing around being bored. I asked for something to do, but the place wasn't well organized so just covering 'the sales floor' was the job, I guess. I hope to find a place where I can be busy and productive. Tell me more about how your office works." Here the answer shows a positive trait and then asks about the job at hand. You need to know what kind of environment you will face once hired, which makes it perfectly fine to ask questions throughout the interview.

115. *"What have you learned from the jobs you've had?"*

"I've learned how important it is to be on time, to be at work every day, and to work hard while I'm there. When I was a waitress, it really made it hard on everyone if another waitress called in sick. One night I had all the tables because both waitresses didn't show up. It was a very high-pressure, intense night. I worked hard and fast but was tremendously overloaded. Anyone else would have quit. But I knew that the employer was counting on me so I worked that night alone. I also learned that it's crucial to make every effort to be at the job *every* day."

116. *"I see you've never had an internship. Why not?"*
"I only wish I had had that opportunity, but I live in a small town and go home each summer since I can live for free with my parents and earn money for college. There really aren't any internship opportunities there. I have worked hard at the jobs I have had. I've learned teamwork, customer-service skills, and I am very reliable."

117. *"How do you think a former boss or professor who knows you well would describe you?" (Situational)*
Sell yourself through your boss's or professor's eyes by saying, "I had Professor MacDonald for two classes, and she would tell you . . ." Then go into your 60 Second Sell. Adding that you're a conscientious, hard worker is always a plus.

118. *"Give me an example of when you've demonstrated your customer-service skills on the job." (Situational)*
"At McDonald's I worked the drive-through window. You need to be polite, accurate, fast, and efficient or the customers can really pile up. I always double-checked the order on the screen, out loud, to confirm it was what the customer wanted. This almost always eliminated mistakes that would make customers angry."

119. *"Give me an example of a time you've worked on a team or in a group." (Situational)*
"As a communications major, I needed to take Advertising 101. An important part of our class grade was a project. We were put into five groups, six per group. I was the team leader and we divided up the workload. One person fell behind and

didn't do the work. Everyone got angry at this person and told me to 'force him' to do it. Instead, I went to my professor and asked for ideas on ways I could motivate my teammate. I thought about my teacher's suggestions and talked it over with the person. It seems he didn't understand how to do the research, so some of us helped him clarify the steps and soon his work was on par with everyone else's. We all ended up with an A, and I'm proud of how we worked together to complete the project and make the grade."

120. *"Give me an example of a problem you had at college and how you solved it." (Situational)*

"I changed my major at the start of my sophomore year to prelaw and needed an economics course, or I'd be a year behind in the core curriculum. The class that fit my schedule was full, so I went to the first three sessions, talked to the professor, and convinced him to let me in so I wouldn't get behind in my prerequisites. Incidentally, I got an A– in that class."

121. *"Name two or three accomplishments that have given you the most satisfaction. Why?"*

Here is a great opportunity to stress two or three points in your 5 Point Agenda. Let's say organizational skills are one point and time management is another. You could respond: "Graduating from college in four years is a big accomplishment for me, and so was getting that A in Statistics. I held a part-time job while attending school, so I often needed to prioritize and plan out my schedule, setting aside time to study and do papers. Statistics was a challenging course for me and required a lot of extra effort. I organized a study group, and I worked on problems every day. I felt pressured by the job, but needed to work to cover tuition costs, so I cut out extra socializing for a few weeks and pulled an A. I felt like my hard work paid off in both cases, and that's been really satisfying."

122. *If you were to open a company what would it be and why?*

I was just at an international HR conference and a dozen recruiters were sitting at a table discussing this question. It's much trickier than it initially appears. The average student simply answered this inquiry by saying that they'd open a company like the one they were at. That response got them a very low score. No creativity, no real thought went into their answer the recruiters said. One recruiter said, "That's the brownnose answer—just telling me what you think I want to hear and you are so wrong." The recruiters revealed that they were looking for originality in the company you'd start. They wanted details, specifics, and forward thinking about a *real* company the student dreamed about. That was the answer that scored the highest. Think of it as if you were making a pitch on the TV show *Shark Tank*. That's the right way to answer this tough one.

Questions for Those with Advanced Degrees:
MAs, MBAs, JDs, MDs, PhDs, or Other Doctorates

123. *"What motivated you to go to law school (or enter the master's or PhD program)?"*

Address where your interest came from and what professional career you hope to have. For example: "I have always loved negotiating and think it's a natural talent. I researched jobs where I could make a career in handling business negotiations and determined that I would be able to do so as an attorney." Another response might be: "After I got out into the business world, I found that my career path at a large company would be difficult without advancing my education. I could not afford to go full-time, so I went into an executive MBA program part-time. I entered, made sacrifices, worked hard at school, and even got promoted while I was attending. I was able to apply some of the class material immediately in my marketing job. Now that I'm finished, I am looking to contribute more than ever before and feel my education will help me to achieve more professionally."

124. *"How would you demonstrate an entrepreneurial mind-set here?"*

This level of performance, initiative, and drive is important to many employers, especially in emerging companies and high-tech. Try to give specific examples that show you as a self-starter, an innovator, or a team leader with creative ideas. Mention how you improved a process, added a new service, organized something, or recognized a trend and contributed solutions to capitalize on it. Demonstrating that you think and act like the business owner is essential.

125. *"Tell me about some of the strategies and actions you have used to build relationships with team members." (Situational)*

They want specific evidence of your leadership ability. Give an example of a project or event or job where you developed good relations with everyone you needed to work with. Mention that you take time to get to know each person and to cultivate an atmosphere of cordial exchange with everyone you work with. Stress your strong communication skills in writing, email, and giving verbal directions. Add that you always try to be resourceful or help out others if there's something you do well that they need support with.

126. *"Tell me about a time when you had to ask for assistance from someone who you didn't think wanted to help you." (Situational)*

Don't expect to be friends with everyone, but you can work hard to build trust and be likable. You could respond: "During my clerkship in the prosecutor's office, the paralegal who was assigned to work with me really resented it. She felt she knew a lot more than I did and was prickly at first. Once I figured it out, I casually went to her and asked if she'd share her knowledge and teach me how to retrieve a report or electronic file. I complimented her on her ability and said I was learning so much from her. I genuinely thanked her. I think most people want to be recognized—my actions thawed this paralegal and we spent the rest of the time working pretty compatibly together."

127. *"What trends do you think are most impacting this field?"*

Be sure you have this answer down pat. The employer is looking to see how well read you are in the field. To stay abreast of industry information, read journals and online articles, attend conferences, and network. Select two or three big trends and be able to clearly define what impact you think they may have. This question is to see how visionary you are, how you digest information, and whether you foresee solutions. To illustrate this, here's an effective approach: "I think that healthcare is in a crisis in America. Doctors are being squeezed from all sides—insurance payments are down, workloads are up, overheads for those in private practice are skyrocketing. I believe more groups will evolve, and more doctors will become hospital employees. There has already been a shift toward hospitals' forming partnerships with specialty groups, and I think this will expand in the years to come. Most of the articles I read and doctors I talk to seem critical of the business-operation side of things. I see more management firms—possible branches of the hospital administration team—running this aspect so doctors can focus on patients. You will definitely see a change in the physician 'on-call' system because the current system is too burdensome for many groups to handle anymore, especially with so many women doctors becoming working parents and wanting more of a family life. Healthcare systems will get tested and rebuilt, and some will crumble as people age and get sicker, technology increases life spans, and costs escalate. I think it's going to be a much-challenged industry over the next dozen years but one with opportunity for those with more entrepreneurial thinking in approaching business solutions." Obviously, such a candidate really knows the field and has analyzed the problems. The employer sees him or her as the person who is going to help shape the industry in the thirty years to come. Demonstrating a solid understanding of trends and industry problems is key.

128. *"Tell us about an app you like and how you'd improve it."*

This question is looking at your creative problem-solving skills. The app you select needs to be one you know well. You should share with them the app (assuming it's on your phone) and show them how it works. It can be a personal interest app—like cooking. Be sure to answer the question on how you would improve it.

Another angle is to discuss a new app you saw advertised, but when you went to download it the app was available only for iPhone and iPad. So you would improve this by making sure it was available in both Android and Apple formats at release, especially if the company was using it in national marketing/advertising campaigns.

Do Your Best

Preparing for potential questions in advance will give you a big advantage over the numerous job hunters who do not prepare. When you write out answers, you have time to analyze the difficult questions and calmly select effective responses that demonstrate to the employer that you can and will do her job well.

Actually, the reason people think questions are tough or difficult is that they haven't really thought about them. They get stumped because they have no plan to follow, no previous ideas jotted down. Short, concise answers of less than 60 seconds that avoid the minefields can result in *you* landing the job. Your interview is really where the employer decides whether or not to hire you. Work hard to do your best. You will not win every time, but you'll improve with each interview and get better at effectively marketing your abilities and convincing employers that *you* are the one to hire.

There are two things to

aim at in life:

first to get what you want

and after that to enjoy it.

Only the wisest of men achieve both.

CHAPTER 8

Salary Questions

The hardest questions can be those that deal with salary. Handled correctly, successful salary negotiations can add thousands of dollars to your new paycheck. Almost as easily, a slip of the tongue can cost you a great deal of money—sometimes even the job itself. Answering all the salary questions like a pro can assure you of obtaining the highest possible offer from an employer. The premise that you must work from is this: whoever mentions money first loses. Don't let it be you!

Secrets of Establishing Your Value

Always, always, always establish your value first. People want what they want. Employers too. When you are the one they want, this psychology becomes your competitive edge in the salary-negotiation process. Once the employer decides they must have you to do the work, there is a role reversal: now they need to recruit and sell *you* on taking the job. It all begins with knowing what your skills and abilities are worth, and then communicating that value to the employer. The end result is that they *must* have you to do the job.

How to Find Out What They Will Pay

To accurately assess your value in the workplace, I suggest you conduct an investigation into what comparable jobs pay in your geographical area. There are several places to find this information. Associations and business magazines frequently publish annual salary surveys. They often break down salary by job title, level of experience, and geographical region. Salary surveys are often published online. The Department of Labor publishes numerous salary lists, or you can ask a reference librarian to help you find the salary information you seek. Last, consider asking colleagues this question: "I'm seeking a new position as a buyer for a national retailer. I have five years' experience. If I ask for a salary of $65,000, do you think that is reasonable? Would it be reasonable for your company?" Another technique is to ask, "What is the typical range this job would pay in your company?" Gather the facts early so you have a reasonable expectation of the salary you could obtain. Be sure to research employers of a similar type and scale— nonprofits and small businesses may pay less than their larger counterparts, though not always.

Salary History Requests

About a quarter of the time, job ads ask you to submit a salary history. Why? This screening tool is simply a starting point to narrow down potential applicants. The best strategy is to simply send nothing. Leave any salary requests blank. Employers have been known to increase the salary, change the job title, add more benefits, and pay thousands more than they initially set forth in order to hire the person they *want* for the job. Job hunters eliminate themselves from consideration not only when their salary history is high but also if it appears to be too low. The employer concludes that the candidate is not as good as the resume says and that he's exaggerating, or even lying, since the employer assumes the applicant should be making more money. A trick some employers use to get you to reveal your salary history is to state in the ad, "Only those who send salary history will be considered." Respond to this in your cover letter by adding a line or two at the end that cites a magazine, journal, association, or online salary survey that offers a range; for example, "A recent issue of *Engineering* magazine's industry salary survey states that a manufacturing engineer like myself, with seven years of experience at a large company, makes between $75,000 and $120,000, and I'm within that range."

The Electronic Application's Salary Box

Online applications can be tricky because most require you to enter a figure. First, try to leave the box empty and see if the online application will process without it—sometimes it does. Many won't. Next try adding a word like "open" or "salary + bonus." If you get an error message, you may need to enter a figure. Use a range like "50s–60s," or a broad number like $100,000+. If you must use a number, use the + sign after a rounded-out salary figure, such as $80,000+ (salary + bonus + perks).

Handling the Probing Recruiter or HR Person

These people are not your friends, no matter how nice they seem. They are paid by the employer, and *they work on behalf of the employer*. So treat them as if you were talking directly to the prospective boss. When questioned about your salary, turn the tables and respond by saying, "What exactly is the range for this job?" Your strategy is to never reveal what you are making or have been paid, because it'll hurt your potential to negotiate later.

Answering the Questions

129. *"What salary do you expect if we offer you the job?"*

Too often, job hunters just throw out a number. That is a critical mistake. Always remember that the first person who mentions money loses—both in terms of real dollars the employer is willing to pay and, in some cases, the job. If you are currently underpaid, you could be screened out completely.

If we use the psychology of people wanting what they want, we must first make the employer want us. Here's where my "salary extractor" technique works well. Answer with, "What is the salary range this position pays?" This volleyball technique encourages them to give you the figure. Typically they will say, "$50,000 to $60,000" or something like "in the nineties." You respond, "I'm within your range," or if it is low, "I'm near that range," and then go on with the interview.

A more persistent interviewer may say, "Well, we need to determine salary expectations before we go on. What figure do you expect?" An effective response might be, "Compensation is directly tied to responsibilities and factors such as overtime needs and travel requirements. I don't think I've gotten enough information about the job yet to determine what is fair. Can we table this question until later?" Often they agree. Another approach: "I expect to be fairly compensated for my work. I feel confident that if we determine I'm the right person to do the job, we can reach an agreement. To me, it's the job itself that is most important." This approach can often detour the employer to move on. And it focuses the interest on their needs, not yours.

Sometimes you get a very persistent recruiter who is pushing you hard to reveal your salary. Try this approach. "I'm certain we're talking about a six-figure job, right?" allows them to agree. "Can we table this conversation until the end so I can hear more about the duties and you can learn more about my skills and experience and we can see if there is really a good match here?" Most times they agree. You can mention that you need to know the demands of the job so you can accurately determine salary needs. It's *critical* to avoid lengthy salary discussions. At this stage in the interview, mention a figure too low and the employer will think you certainly must lack the skills to do the job and that you exaggerated on your resume. If you are too high, they'll think you'd never work for less. The interviewer will quickly determine you are not the one they want—based on these answers alone.

Your winning strategy is to keep the conversation centered on how well you can do the job. Continually sell your 5 Point Agenda. Utilize your 60 Second Sell whenever appropriate. These will market your best strengths and influence the employer to decide he *must* have you. Once the job offer has been formally made, *then* it's the right time to discuss and negotiate the salary you want and deserve for performing the job.

130. *"What is your current salary?"*
This usually makes people nervous and then they reveal their salary. *Wrong answer.* You'll only be able to negotiate the best salary if the employer is kept wondering. Once the employer decides they want to hire you, they switch mental gears from screening you out to wanting to recruit you and fearing you won't take the job. This is the position you need to be in. When pushed for a salary figure, keep this fact in mind. Hundreds of hiring managers have admitted to me that they rarely offer the highest salary they are willing to pay as the first offer. So when they hear a candidate's current salary, they only offer

5% to 10% more, realizing people will take it. These employers *had* more dollars budgeted that they could pay, but since they got the new person "cheap," they redirect the extra money to another budget item.

Be prepared. Respond with: "Well, what I was paid previously was based on job duties, and I am sure you offer a competitive wage, but I still don't have a clear idea of what the job duties, managerial level, travel requirements, overtime, etc., will be. I need to get more information before we discuss the value I bring and what compensation package is fair for these duties." Another effective solution is to note a salary survey that defined the salary range for people with your skills in a company of similar size, adding that salary, bonuses, benefits, and vacation all affect your decision, and you'd be happy to go into detail when you are offered the job.

Relocation Situations

If you are moving to take the job, you might get grilled about the cost of moving. Companies vary dramatically when it comes to the relocation packages they offer. You need to be savvy as to what is reasonable. It's a rare company nowadays that will buy your house after the last major housing crash left too many people with houses worth less than what they owe. Some relocation packages offer to pay a lump sum to relocate, which you use to move yourself. Others are very generous but have strict payback rules if you quit before a required length of time (usually one to two years) has passed. Expect to be asked several questions on this topic. Usually HR will go over these details to be certain that moving is still a viable option for you. It is wise to tread carefully in discussing this early on—gather facts, but wait for the majority of this conversation until *after* you have been offered the job. Relocation packages can be negotiated, added to, and improved from the "standard offer," so waiting until the offer is on the table is advisable.

131. *"We have a relocation package since you'll need to move here. Do you own a home?"*

If you do, then answer, "Yes, how does your relocation package work?" Let them explain the details about moving costs and assistance with real estate issues, since housing can vary widely from region to region. You might interject that you plan to look at real estate when you're interviewing in the new location. They may have already set this up for you. If not, now is a wise time to ask if they will connect you to a real estate agent, and then move on with the interview.

132. *"Does your spouse work?"*

This is an acceptable question since a spousal job can dramatically affect whether you can move. They may or may not offer career assistance to your spouse. Some employers have an HR person offer help; others hire a local career counselor. The key is that the employer is trying to determine if you'll really move, or if your spouse's situation will be a problem. Sometimes they offer to give your spouse a position if their skills fit something available in the company. Very large organizations such as colleges and universities are more likely to do this. The correct approach is to reaffirm that you are willing to move. "We have discussed this career opportunity and my husband (or wife) is in full agreement that it's a great move for our family." Employers love to hear you are moving to be closer to family, so if this is accurate in your case, mention that fact too.

133. *"Have you looked into the cost of living in this area?"*

Many places, such as New York, San Francisco, Los Angeles, Boston, Honolulu, and Seattle, are very expensive. Housing costs can be exorbitant, especially if you come from an area where the cost of living is low and a $250,000 home is a mansion. In some areas, livable homes begin at more than one million dollars. Do your homework before the interview. Go online and use relocation tools that show what your income needs to be in the new location and what housing will cost. Reply to this question by saying you have done some investigation and understand that the housing costs are higher, but the professional options and the cultural opportunities make this a very attractive situation. Many companies worry about spending a lot of time with you only to have you turn down the job because of how expensive it is to live in the area. You should be certain you will move and might politely inquire about whether the company offers COLAs, the HR term for cost-of-living adjustments. Before you readily agree that you'd love to move, research the option thoroughly.

I warn you that many people make big mistakes here. A client who was a CEO was recruited for a job in Aspen, Colorado. It was a winter wonderland with pristine snow, clear mountain air, and sunny blue skies. The employer even offered a $400,000 forgivable housing loan since homes were so costly. The CEO moved his family. Six months later I got a call saying that no one was happy there. They disliked their daughter's new school. The wife didn't fit into the resort social life and was terribly lonely. The cost of everything from groceries to clothes to meals out was shockingly, astronomically high. The whole family was miserable. The client quit and moved back to his previous location with no job and no prospects. Learn from his mistake—look really carefully before you move.

*B*eyond today lie your
highest aspirations. You may not
reach them, but you can always
believe in them and try to follow
where they lead.

CHAPTER 9

Questions You Should Ask

At some point in every interview the employer will ask, "Do you have any questions?" This is your opportunity to determine that this job, company, and boss are a good place for you. Often the candidate searches to ask almost anything, appearing dumb to the interviewer because he did not prepare his own list of questions in advance. This will not happen to you. Take the time before the interview to think about what information you need to aid you in deciding if the job is a good fit for you. This is a very important part of the interviewing process. The employer often puts a lot of weight on what you ask. People have a hard time thinking up their questions. The questions you want to ask are strictly job related and duty related. You can ask all about the company's benefits, sick leave, and pension programs *after* you've gotten the job offer.

How to Impress the Employer

Hiring managers repeatedly tell me that they pay particular attention to the questions that applicants ask them. Your questions, especially when they are insightful, send a signal that you are not only interested in the job but truly trying to evaluate whether this will be a good match and work out long term for both parties. A top manager at AT&T said: "I judge candidates by the questions they ask. That's what's most revealing to me. I want someone focused on succeeding in the job and not just centered on how much money I will pay him."

Before the interview, prepare a list of pertinent questions that you would like answered to determine if this position is really a good job for you. Write or type out your questions on a piece of paper that you can take out when it's your turn to ask questions. The employer is impressed that you cared enough about the position to think through his organization's needs and duties. Do not bring up any questions about salary or benefits at this time. Focus on determining if you want to do this job. Your questions also give insight into your thoroughness when given important responsibilities. Ten to fifteen questions are a reasonable number to have on your list. Many will have been answered during the interview. Bring up anything the employer mentioned that you want to know more about. If by chance he has already answered every question, say this: "As I check over my list, my questions on your software were covered as well as the equipment you use. We discussed budgets and training policies. I guess you've covered everything already."

Gaining Insight into the Corporate Culture

Every organization has a workplace environment that defines what it is actually like to work there. Before you meet the employer, do some research. Check out the hiring manager on LinkedIn. Go to www.glassdoor.com and read what others say who work for this particular company. Network with friends to get some insider information as to what is going on in the company and department you are applying to.

Prior to the interview, you may have preconceived ideas about the company's culture based on its marketing and advertising or on media news. Often these preconceived ideas prove to be inaccurate once you get into the interview and begin to ask your questions. Better to learn now that you don't want this job, rather than three weeks after you've started. Therefore pay close attention to the answers and whether this is a boss you would like to work with daily.

You can't always have prepared all your questions in advance since they often arise as a result of some part of the interview. It's often best to ask these questions as soon as they come up, saying, "Could you explain that more fully?" or "Please elaborate." Be sure you get answers to incongruities and investigate if a red flag comes up. Use your detective skills to determine what the true workplace environment will be and if it's a comfortable fit for you.

37 Questions You Could Ask

Here are 37 questions that you can consider asking. Notice how each one is designed to gather details about doing the job and to learn more about the organization's work culture and environment. Be sure to pose the appropriate question to the correct person. Technical questions and job specifics are unlikely to be answered by the HR person, whose responsibility is to screen and validate your true experience, but who possesses only a general idea of the job duties. By the end of your questions with the hiring manager or decision maker you should know whether or not you want to work there.

- *"Could you describe to me your typical management style and the type of employee that works well with you?"*
- *"What are the day-to-day responsibilities I'll have in this job?"*

- *"Whom will I be supervising?"*
- *"Could you explain your organizational structure to me?"*
- *"What is the organization's plan for the next five years, and how does this department or division fit in?"*
- *"Will we be expanding, bringing on any new products or new services that I should be aware of?"*
- *"What are some of the skills and abilities you see as necessary for someone to succeed in this job?"*
- *"What challenges might I encounter if I take on this position?"*
- *"What are your major concerns that need to be immediately addressed in this job?"*
- *"What are the areas in the job that you'd like to see improved upon?"*
- *"What is your company's policy on providing seminars, workshops, and training so the employees can keep up on their skills or acquire new skills?"*
- *"What is the budget this department operates with? Has it been changed in the last year, and if yes, how?"*
- *"Are there any restraints or cutbacks planned that would decrease that budget?"*
- *"What particular computer equipment and software do you use here? When was your last upgrade?"*
- *"Are any new equipment purchases planned?"*
- *"What personality traits do you think are necessary to succeed in this job?"*
- *"Will I be working as part of a team or alone?"*
- *"What committees will I participate in?"*
- *"How will my leadership responsibilities and performance be measured? By whom?"*
- *"To what extent are the functions of this department considered important by upper management?"*
- *"Are there any weaknesses in the department that you are working to improve?"*
- *"What are the company's long-term goals?"*

- *"What are the department's goals, and how do they fit into the company's mission?"*
- *"What are the company's strengths and weaknesses compared with its competition?"*
- *"How does the reporting structure work here? What are acceptable channels of communication?"*
- *"What new endeavors is the company currently undertaking?"*
- *"What goals or objectives need to be achieved in the next six months? Next year?"*
- *"What areas of the job would you like to see improvement in with regard to the person who was most recently performing these duties?"*
- *"Would I encounter any coworker or staff person who's proved to be a problem in the past? If yes, please explain."*
- *"Describe the atmosphere of the office."* (With this question, you are looking for clues on pressure and stress level.)
- *"What types of people seem to excel here?"*
- *"Is the company quick or slow to adopt new technology?"*
- *"How would you describe the politics of this organization?"*
- *"Can you give me an idea of the typical workload and extra hours or special needs it demands?"*
- *"Where is the person who previously held this job?"* (If fired, ask why; if promoted, where he or she went; if it is a newly created job, get a better idea of why it was added.)
- *"How does the company promote personal and professional growth?"*
- *"How would you describe the corporate culture here?"*

Ideally, you need to stay focused on the job—the duties and/or the promotional opportunities. Remember, a key strategy is to not ask questions about salary, benefits, or perks. The best time to cover those issues is *after* you've been offered the job.

Success can be yours,
but nothing happens by itself.
It will all come your way
once you understand
that you have to make it
come your way
by your own efforts.
When opportunity knocks,
be ready.

CHAPTER 10

Negotiating the Best Deal

As the employer says, "You got the job," you mumble some pleasantry as you silently scream *YES!* As tempting as it is to accept then and there, if you intend to negotiate for any benefits or salary increase I advise you to refrain from that outburst and say, "I'd like to meet with you tomorrow and discuss your offer and all the details." If they haven't stated the salary, ask it. Arrange the meeting time. If you are on the phone, end the conversation. If it's via email, reply by asking to discuss the specifics and offer a day and time. If you are meeting face-to-face, try to meet again the next day if possible. Be sure you are talking with the hiring manager—not negotiating with an HR person.

You have a lot of preparation to do, especially if you want the employer to raise the offer. This meeting you just arranged is called the "negotiations interview," and there is a formula to follow to successfully negotiate a better compensation package.

Negotiating effectively has a major impact over your earning lifetime. Individuals who remained in a company for more than three years would typically not be getting the larger raises. They usually get small, incremental increases in the 2–5% range. Significant raises happen when someone moves on to a new employer and negotiates a large salary increase. Those salary jumps, according to salary surveys, when going to a new employer are usually 17% above an individual's previous job salary. The Society of Human Resources Management just released a rather shocking survey result. It noted that over the course of the person's career, anyone who didn't negotiate for a higher salary every time they started a new job would actually earn $500,000 to $1,000,000 LESS in lifetime income than an individual who was savvy when handling their salary compensation package, ensuring big increases.

Men and Women Negotiate Differently

Women still make 23% less than men, according to the Department of Labor. This number has remained constant over the last decade and shows little evidence of changing. Much of this discrepancy is due to the fact that men often try to negotiate their salary, whereas women typically accept the original offer as given. Client after client after client has proven that they can improve the original offer by following the negotiation strategies that follow. What typically happens, though, is that when Lora is offered a new job, she accepts the starting salary of $58,000, but when Jack is offered the exact same job, he negotiates. Jack accepts $70,000—a 21% difference. All future raises are based on the beginning salary, so it will likely take Lora *four years* of raises to reach Jack's starting salary. And since bonuses and raises are calculated from the salary figure, Jack's raises will push him further ahead of Lora faster, since he began at a higher compensation level. Women, therefore, must change their thinking from the sociologically ingrained "be polite, be humble, be grateful, be a pleaser" to acting like a competitive candidate who expects to earn top dollar and benefits in exchange for her talents.

Mental Preparation Is Essential

Many people talk themselves out of negotiating for a higher salary or benefits. Their self-talk is based on fear or insecurity. You need to have the right mind-frame. Ask yourself these questions: *Are you a mediocre worker? Are you above average compared with others who do your job?* The answer is yes you are a better worker and no you are *not* mediocre. Therefore, you offer the employer more value than the next person. So think about that and how you will do a great job for this employer. Then tell yourself you deserve to be paid the maximum amount this employer is willing to extend for this job. You owe it to your family (or self) to try to obtain the highest salary possible. You have great value to offer and must *think* that you are valuable to the employer. Keep telling yourself this fact. With that in mind, *ask* for what you want. More money, and/or more perks.

The Biggest Raises Come with a New Job

The biggest salary increases are almost always the result of changing jobs and companies. These raises can range from 15% to 30% above the previous salary. Some clients have seen 40% to 50% increases, and a few actually doubled their salaries. Many people use the new job as an opportunity to move up into a higher-level position and secure more money. Being underpaid is a common reason for leaving a job, and when you pursue an opportunity to move on to a new organization, you should expect it to be a very profitable endeavor.

More Employers Are Negotiating the Whole Compensation Package

Employers are now showing more latitude in negotiating salaries than ever before. They typically start low, but have the latitude to raise it—often significantly—if you are savvy and negotiate. It seems as though thousands of dollars and extra perks such as more vacation and signing bonuses are there for the asking. One CEO summed it up this way: "People are more aware of their value these days, and it's a struggle to find good people. Although many may be looking, few can help propel us forward. We must offer a competitive salary to retain talent to allow our organization to thrive. What's a few thousand more if they are the perfect match for the job?" Moral of the story—ASK.

Understanding Pay Scales

Salary negotiation is a game—a sophisticated game but a game nonetheless. You must enter this arena fully equipped with facts, figures, and influential information. *Asking* for more compensation properly rarely risks an offer being withdrawn, but *demanding* more can. Therefore, begin by analyzing the employer's situation.

Step 1: Assess the employer's compensation style.

Fixed Offer. Some employers simply do not negotiate. They offer a take-it-or-leave-it deal. They have a set limit on how much that job is worth to them. This is particularly true with smaller employers or large companies handling entry-level jobs.

Pay Grade System. A predetermined range is set for the job, based on the duties and responsibilities required. Where you fall in this range is determined by your years of experience. This system rarely offers the top salary to anyone. Instead, the top is the level earned in raises over the years. To significantly raise the salary, the employer often has to reclassify the job in a higher pay grade. This has been known to happen, especially when it has been established that the employer underestimated the skills necessary to adequately perform the job.

Negotiable Guidelines. This is the best situation. The employer has more liberty to raise or lower the salary as he sees fit. This allows you the best chance to bargain for your services.

Step 2: Assess the job market's supply of qualified candidates.

If there are others who are equally qualified and the employer would be happy with any of them, your negotiating power may be reduced. Then again, I've seen clients sail through stacks of resumes from four hundred potential employees and go right to the top, succeeding, after nine hours of interviewing, in being offered the job. The employer really wanted them and even though some were unemployed at the time, they were able to secure excellent compensation packages in spite of the competition. They argued that they were the best of the lot. The employer agreed and paid dearly to have them join their team.

*Step 3: Determine what a fair offer is before you begin
the face-to-face negotiations.*

Predetermine a fair, reasonable goal for both you and the employer. This is critical if you've been overpaid or underpaid. During your salary research, you should have defined what a fair price is. When leaving a large Fortune 500 company for a much smaller organization, the offers might be less. On the other hand, having spent years just getting cost-of-living raises (typically 3–6%), you may find that you now earn less than the going market rate. When moving from an underpaid situation, ask yourself how much more is enough, and know the answer before you begin to negotiate.

10 Negotiation Strategies

During the negotiation interview, implement these ten techniques in your efforts to get the best deal. By using the negotiation strategies that follow, you can get what you want (maybe even much more than you'd hoped for).

1. *Use a Confident Approach*
Your tone often affects the results of this whole process. Exude enthusiasm for the job. Reconfirm your ability to do the job well. Have a win-win attitude. To begin the conversation, ask about medical benefits, vacations, and travel requirements. Grill them on all these terms. Find out if they offer other perks, such as health club memberships, tuition reimbursement, and day care subsidies. Ask about overtime policies and what is actually practiced. Oftentimes, the policy is that you receive compensation time for your overtime hours, but the practice is that you are absolutely discouraged from ever using it. Learn about the company rules and practices.

2. *Focus on the Employer's Needs*
Continually resell yourself throughout this process. Reaffirm the reasons they want you, the skills you'll bring, and how you'll solve their problems. Mention your 60 Second Sell and stress how quickly you will be productive. In other words, give them reasons to pay you more. This is an important strategy because the interviewer may need to go to their boss and the

personnel department to obtain the approval to grant a higher salary. When you offer them ammunition, such as, "My experience with your systems is an asset and will save a lot of time since I already know the software," they can better persuade their boss and come back with a higher offer.

Stress the job needs, your abilities to do the job, and what your contributions will be.

3.   Use a Negotiation Lead-in Statement

To break into the discussion about salary, say, "I'm really interested in the position. I was a little disappointed that the offer was lower than I expected, especially since I have this experience or these skills (note something specific) and will come up to speed quickly." Then be quiet and remain quiet while the employer makes the next move. Another approach is to say, "I'm very interested in the job, and we are close to my salary needs; is there a possibility of negotiating here?" Smile and follow the employer's lead.

4.   Negotiate to Get the Money Up Front

Cash shall always remain king. Promised bonuses, raises, stock options, and reviews in a few months all have a way of never happening down the line. Every dollar you negotiate into the salary base is more money you can spend on things you and your family want. Work toward the extra money up front. These negotiations could give you in minutes what would take years to achieve with raises.

5.   Try

Most people, especially women and unemployed people, are afraid to try. Women by nature devalue themselves. They don't recognize their full worth in the workplace and rarely demand it. Salary studies still reveal that women are paid substantially less than men because women allow it. I encourage every person to expect and seek comparable compensation for the job performed. One client sounded shocked when she called to say that she followed my techniques to the letter and the employer offered her $9,000 more. She was astounded, but she wouldn't have been if she had more self-confidence about her value as a marketable employee.

The unemployed person typically feels that he or she sits in a difficult spot. They often need the job and the employer knows it. In this situation, first reiterate what you bring to the employer. Try to get fair compensation. Oftentimes, the employer will start with a lowball offer just to see if you will take it. Test the waters to see if there is room for them to pay more. There almost always is. If you've been actively interviewing, it doesn't hurt to mention that there are other companies interested in your talents.

6. *Be Specific When It Counts*

The employer may ask you what figure you have in mind. Try this: "According to all the salary survey data, someone with my ten years of experience would be in the upper seventies." They may ask for the number; then reveal what you want: "I was thinking $78,000 is what I'd accept." Be willing to wait. They may need to go back and ask HR or their boss to get the additional dollars. If they want you, they'll be your advocate and almost always come back with more than they originally offered.

7. *Don't Forget to Negotiate the Perks*

Compensation benefits come in very complex packages, from nothing at all to free day-care services, health-club memberships, dry-cleaning, and pizza. Consider the extra value a company's retirement plan adds—some are great and others offer nothing at all. What about vacation time, flexible hours, tuition reimbursement, fewer hours, days off, relocation ex-

penses, stock options, a company car, expense accounts, bonuses? Perhaps the salary cannot be raised, but additional
benefits could be added.

Vacations and days off can often be negotiated. Be careful
because other staff often resent favoritism to a new employee.
And just because you had five weeks of vacation at your last
company (with ten years of service), it is unlikely the new company will give you five. Be reasonable, but do inquire if there's
anything more they can do. Employers often respond by offering an additional week or two.

Look closely at the medical plan. What kind of coverage is
provided? What deductibles does the plan include? Who pays
for dependents? If you pay, what will that cost be? Many companies' health plans offer lousy coverage with $5,000 to $10,000
deductibles every year. My clients have successfully argued for
a higher salary to compensate for switching medical plans when
their old employer had better insurance or covered the entire
family with a tiny co-pay, and the new one covers just the employee. Additionally, if you or a family member has a chronic
illness, check with the new company's insurer to be certain
your medications and doctors are covered before you accept the
job, as these expenses can become exorbitant if you must pay
them once you enter the new plan.

Stock options are real money if you are granted a block of
stock and they trade above your strike price. See stock as a nice
extra but don't accept it in lieu of salary. *Cash is, and always will
be, king.*

Relocation packages come in all prices and sizes—everything
from $10,000 up to all moving, real estate, and temporary living
expenses. Listen to what's offered, and find out what your length
of employment must be to avoid paying all the money back.
There is usually some latitude to cover more costs, so if the employer is being conservative or stingy, this is a good place to ask
for more financial assistance.

Predetermine which benefits are important to you and negotiate for them.

8. *Practice*

Think through the negotiation interview. Visualize a successful outcome. Then ask a friend to role-play the interview with you. Defend why you are worth the money. Listen to the feedback—did you convince them? This preparation will decrease your anxiety and increase your confidence.

9. *Know Your Bottom Line*

Only you can decide when the offer is too low. There will be other offers, but they may be weeks down the road. Never ever bluff the potential employer. Offers can be withdrawn when a job hunter says, "$66,000 is as low as I will accept." Be prepared to keep looking. Sometimes that is the right move for you. Decide on the lowest figure you can reasonably accept, one that will cover your bills and allow you to concentrate on succeeding in the job and not immediately start looking for another, higher-paying one.

10. *Get an Employment Letter*

Once you have agreed upon all the terms, ask for an employment letter. You can offer to write it or the employer can, but be sure the employer signs it. This letter should outline all the terms of your employment, covering salary, signing bonuses, stock options, starting date, benefits, and particularly noting anything different from the organization's normal policies. Too many promises are made and quickly forgotten once you start the job. Get the details in writing so there are no misunderstandings later. People who have failed to do so have suffered when the promised extra week of vacation was "forgotten" once they started. A written agreement protects what you've negotiated for. These letters are very common, and it's wise to obtain one.

Inquiry About a Signing Bonus

Signing bonuses are once again very popular. Executives can almost always ask for these. Professionals with sought-after skillsets in high-tech, manufacturing, legal, and health care are likely to secure one. Oftentimes, you can ask and receive one no matter what industry or field you are in. Even nonprofits sometimes offer this one-time perk. Signing bonuses can range from $3,000 to $25,000, with $5,000 or $10,000 being most common. You almost always have to ask to get this bonus, but employers often say yes, so it's wise to ask if a signing bonus is an option you can receive.

What to Do with Multiple Offers

Oh, the luxury of choices. Be *sure* there is another choice. Once a firm offer is made, job hunters become convinced that the other job for which they just interviewed will bring an offer, too. Will it? Employers don't like to be pushed just because you have "other opportunities." A straightforward approach works best. Call the other employers with whom you interviewed and tell them you have a firm offer. Explain that you still have a strong interest in their job. Ask them for a status report. Tell them your timeline and wait. If they are going to make you a firm offer, they will contact you within that time limit. Sometimes, you are not their first choice and they will say so. Either way, you will know where you stand. A job in hand is a real job—not a hope, dream, or belief. Make your decision based on facts, not wishful thinking.

When two solid offers stand, create a pros-and-cons chart for each job. Then decide which one you want, and negotiate hard for the best terms they can offer, making them aware that they are bidding against another company for your services.

How It Works

I continually hear from clients, seminar participants, and job hunters who've read this book, saying how they've successfully negotiated a better compensation package. Many are able to get a signing bonus simply by saying, "What about a signing bonus?"

When Michael was reluctant to accept a promising job offer, he shared his reservations with the hiring manager: "If I stay at my current job, I've got a major $30,000 bonus due on January 1. I'm tempted to take your job, but this is a significant stumbling block. Could I maybe get some kind of signing bonus?" The result was a $20,000 signing bonus and $10,000 more in stock on arrival.

Jessica told a potential employer, "Considering my twelve years of expertise in major event planning, I thought your offer was a little on the low side." She admitted to me that remaining quiet was then the hardest thing she'd ever done. The employer responded: "Oh, I know we can do better. Personnel makes us offer a low-end figure just to see if you'll take it—many do, you know." The next morning when the employer called back, Jessica was $6,000 richer.

Sometimes the salary's acceptable but the benefits, particularly vacation or medical insurance, are not. And although many employers have set vacation benefits, you can usually get more. This happened in Bob's case, at a large healthcare facility where the salary was what he'd expected but not the vacation. He phrased his concern this way: "Your salary is in the range of what I expected. But after having twenty-five vacation days these last several years, it's a long reach to go back to just ten. It seems to me, ten days is great for a beginner in the field, but as a professional with all the experience and accomplishments I bring to the table, I'd need vacation to rejuvenate and recharge my batteries from the stress these jobs entail, and ten days seems too much of a slip backward." They responded: "What do you think is fair?" And Bob replied, "In my mind, eighteen to twenty days is fair."

The employer had a reputation for being bureaucratic and rigid, and yet they surprised us both when they came back with eighteen days off. Bob took the job and has been a great asset to them since. Incidentally, the salary was a very nice bump up, too.

John was worried about changing jobs after he learned the new company had a large, $5,000 medical deductible. His wife had a chronic illness and this would be a big out-of-pocket hit for him to absorb. He mentioned this concern to the hiring manager, who came back with an $8,000 salary increase, and John accepted the new position.

Sandra graduated from a good college and began looking for a social-work job. She interviewed with a small agency and was thrilled when they offered her the job until she learned how low the salary was. She consulted with me after her best efforts were met with the response, "This is all we can pay for the job." Sandra really liked the position and the boss, who had a good reputation as an excellent social worker. I pointed out to Sandra that in her first job after college, working under a boss who would teach her a lot would be a valuable asset in launching her career. She took the job, and under the boss's tutelage has become a good social worker herself. Two years later, she has just moved on to a great new job, ahead of her friends, and negotiated a significant salary increase this time around. When making decisions, it's important to consider what is best for your career and your long-term happiness, and to use that as a decision-making guideline.

Tim was frantic when he lost his job. He did not want to relocate, and he knew it would be very challenging to find a new job in his field since few were available where he lived. He came to me desperate and certain he'd need to take a drop in pay, starting at the bottom in a new field. I proved him wrong. We rewrote his resume, polished his interview skills, and he landed a new position that was a career change. He very reluctantly tried salary negotiations because the offer was higher than the old job, and he assumed he had little to persuade them with. We worked on the psychological obstacles that stopped him from asking for more salary. He followed the strategy we'd outlined, noting his strengths, planning, and managerial experience. Tim's move resulted in a $16,000 salary raise! Not bad for ten minutes of conversation.

In summary, your five keys to salary negotiation success are:

- Know your value in the current workplace
- Ask for a fair price
- Continually sell yourself and reiterate your worth
- Never mention money first
- Evaluate the entire opportunity before deciding: your long-term goals, career growth, job security, etc.

*Some people may succeed
because they are destined to,
but most people succeed
because they are determined to.*

CHAPTER 11

13 Types of Interviews

When the employer calls to say, "We'd like you to come in for an interview," it's important to respond with three questions. First say, "Certainly, may I ask what dates and times you have available?" You are probing to determine how many people they are talking to. Try to be the first or last person they interview. When you are sandwiched between others, the interviews often get hurried, with less time for important notes in between. Plus the interviewer gets bored. At the end of a day, you must show enthusiasm and smile warmly, since the interviewer may be tired.

The next question to ask is about the type of interview. You want to gather as much information as possible. Try, "Whom will I be interviewing with?" Note the interviewer's name and title. Ask for the correct spelling of the hiring manager's name. Probe to see if the person on the phone will share more information about the job duties. Ask if a complete job description is available. If yes, have it emailed to aid you in your preparation. Finally, get clear directions to the office, and inquire about parking if you plan to drive.

Here are some insights to help you deal with the various types of interviews you might encounter.

Telephone Screening Interview

This initial contact is designed to narrow the pool of acceptable candidates and determine whom to call in for a full face-to-face interview. This is very popular these days, and you should expect to be thoroughly grilled when they call. The interviewer seeks to weed out the unqualified and overpriced. The caller can be your potential boss, a member of the HR team, or a recruiter. You must pass this screening or you are out of the running.

This type of phone interview puts you at a major disadvantage because the interviewer knows they will catch you off guard. They often call in the evenings or on weekends. I've personally conducted a lot of these for employers, and I'm amazed at how many people say it is okay to talk when there is obviously a TV on, loud children around, and distracting events going on. Preparation is the key to success, and this screening is the first hurdle along the way. When you get this call, tell the person you are just finishing something and ask if you can call them back in five or ten minutes. Hopefully, you are prepared and have your resume and cover letters close by. Find a quiet spot, get your resume out, and think about the questions they will ask. If you have written out answers to possible questions, get those in front of you too. The employer's objective is to clarify experience and salary expectations. Mentally rehearse your answers. Have a pen and paper in front of you. Jot down the caller's name and take notes as they ask you questions. Smile, so your voice sounds friendly. Their job is to screen and validate applicants' backgrounds. They need to hear that you have the experience to do the job. Demonstrate that you do, with answers that offer examples of your past performance, and reiterate your 5 Point Agenda. Be concise—keep answers to less than 60 seconds, and above all sound interested and enthusiastic about the job. The worst thing you can do is to sound uninterested or dull, with a monotone voice. Be careful to skillfully handle the tricky questions about salary and any work gaps, etc. Follow the salary-negotiation techniques outlined in chapters 8 and 10, because the worst thing you can do is tell the interviewer what your salary is (or was) and they will likely ask you about it during this conversation.

HR/Recruiter Interview

It's become more common to do this interview on the phone, though a few companies still use a face-to-face meeting to conduct the screening. They will review your background. Executive recruiters typically want to account for every moment of your professional existence. They also want salary info and will try to assess whether you have the background and skills to meet all the company's requirements. Be confident, but keep this a two-way conversation. Ask lots of questions about the job, the duties, location, travel requirements, and also about the company and its culture.

Internal HR people (which at many large companies are internal recruiters) are looking to see if you have the skills and experience. They want to clarify and get more details. Using specific examples from past jobs is very useful since it paints a picture for the HR person so they know you can do the work. The big disadvantage is that the HR person is often not specifically familiar with all the details of the job. They are generalists and seek to validate job experience, not job potential. Be sure to structure your answers to demonstrate how you have done the work in the past. Your 60 Second Sell will be effective in outlining your strengths. These interviews usually last about twenty to thirty minutes. To move to the next level, you must convince this person that you *can* do the job. Prepare accordingly, and ask good questions to see if this is a job you even want.

Screening interviews are important as they eliminate those who are flaky, don't have experience, or have salary expectations that are too high or low. Know how to handle those questions, and smile at your phone since they can hear that tone in your voice and it makes you sound more likable.

Hiring Interview

This is a face-to-face, one-on-one interview. This format allows you to build rapport and establish a base to judge your potential boss, who is most often the person conducting the interview. The person may be a well-trained interviewer, as is typical in large, progressive companies. More often, the person has no formal interview training and may ask irrelevant questions or talk too long. Always help him by offering leading information. A client interviewed with a manager who spent twenty minutes talking about the job. She took notes. She asked questions and then used the information to vary one aspect of her 60 Second Sell. Another client exclaimed that it seemed like the interviewer would never let her speak. After thirty minutes, she offered this comment, nodding her head in agreement: "I understand why customer-service skills are so important to you. In my last position, I rewrote our customer-service policy. My research supported the facts that our clients were dissatisfied with busy phone lines and untrained staff. I implemented a new system that answered calls more quickly. Then I developed an employee training program and a manual for daily use on the job. We saw a vast improvement over this last year. What do you feel needs to be done here?" If nothing else, this person took control and showed the employer that she heard his concerns and understood and could solve his problems. It's sometimes necessary to direct the questioning to your strengths, where you can demonstrate solutions as this client did.

All one-on-one interviews require a firm handshake, a smile, continuous eye contact, enthusiasm, and a rapport-building demeanor—open and self-confident, sending the message that you can solve the employer's problems and do the job.

Second Interview

This is usually either with the same person or with someone else in upper management, usually the first interviewer's boss. You may also have arrived here after a panel interview, and now face the decision maker.

You have gathered information at the first interview and should be clear about the employer's true needs. Often, only two or three top candidates remain for this position. Prepare and adjust your 60 Second Sell, with answers to address the employer's true needs. Refer whenever possible to something the interviewer noted in the first meeting. Show enthusiasm and give examples. Bring work samples you can leave behind. The employer wants to get to know you better. He wants to learn about you and your personality, and to determine if he still likes you. He wants to confirm whether you are the best fit available. He is also assessing your potential by examining your past initiative and any new skills you acquired. Work to assure him you are the one—examples and work samples are key here. Demonstrate an understanding of his needs and how you can offer solutions.

The boss's boss looks at the hiring process more globally. How do you fit into the big picture? Will you be promotion material? Are you flexible, adaptable, willing to become the worker they need today and tomorrow? Some worry that you will want a promotion too soon, when their objective is to get someone to stay and do the job they are hiring for. You must show your ability to meet company goals and to be productive and easy to work with. You absolutely must convince this person that you can do the job and are very willing to do it. Show enthusiasm for the position and pride in your past accomplishments. Ask questions about the company's future and how the job and the division fit into the company's short- and long-term goals.

Multiple Interviews

Key positions—CEOs, vice presidents, presidents, executive directors, CFOs, sales managers, human resource directors, administrators, IT managers, marketing and advertising directors—often go through a lengthy, multi-meeting process. So do many middle-management jobs. You will most likely meet several team members and key executives, and the process may take six to ten hours. Companies feel that this extensive courtship time allows them to uncover both your strengths and your true weaknesses, and to determine whether or not they can live with you and your failings. A challenge in this process is that each person often has a slightly different agenda. Try to analyze each person by job title and predetermine his or her concerns. Think about how you would interact with each of them, and prepare answers and your 60 Second Sell accordingly. Many companies also have you meet with your potential staff. They put a lot of weight on the staff comments, so be open and friendly with any staff. Clearly explain what you are like as a manager and listen to what they like. Stress that you treat everyone fairly. Watch for any workplace disharmonies—they are often a red flag that there is a staff conflict. Try not to discuss them in the interview; just reiterate that you treat people fairly. You may feel that this tension is a reason you do not want to pursue the job. If you are still interested, you should wait to discuss and learn about the staff conflicts until the negotiation interview, where you can gain direction from top management on their expectations about how to deal with the problem.

Panel Interview

This type of interview is often challenging because it is difficult to determine who has the ultimate decision-making power, not to mention that it is intimidating to face several people with varying agendas and questions. Topics easily switch from one question to another, limiting the flow and rapport that is easier to create when you're speaking to only one person.

If possible, try to determine who has the final decision-making power and always address that person's needs and concerns above all. Typically, this will be your potential boss—always be certain you know which person that is. If it's not stated at your introduction to the group, ask before the questions start. Create your answers and your 60 Second Sell as if you were speaking only to this person.

There will be times when you will not know who is the true decision maker. Address your answers to the group, but focus your answers in relation to what you think your boss and her boss's needs will be.

When you enter the room, if possible, shake hands firmly and smile as you are introduced to each person. Mention their names. If a table separates you, nod as you greet each person by name, such as, "Hello, Tom," "Nice to meet you, Mary," "Bob." Address the answer to the person who asks the question. They are most interested in your response, so keep your eyes on them while answering. Be sure to answer the question asked. Qualify the question if you want more information before you answer. Look directly at the person as you respond. Good eye contact with the person asking the question is vital during this entire process.

Group Interview

This is a screening interview often used by employers when numerous applicants must be seen to determine a candidate's potential. You will be interviewed along with several other candidates at the same time. The airlines commonly use this type of interview when hiring flight attendants. The purpose is twofold. First, do you meet the physical requirements for the job, such as height, weight, and physical agility? Next, how outgoing, comfortable, and confident are you in a group situation? Because this process is designed to determine those with poor communication and interpersonal skills, practice speaking clearly, firmly, and with a friendly tone. Don't be surprised when you get only a couple of opportunities to answer questions. Radiate confidence that you can effectively deal with the demanding public and that you are cool, calm, and collected in high-pressure situations. These traits are imperative to doing the job well, and this intimidating format seems to aid the employer in a speedy elimination process.

Breakfast, Lunch, or Dinner Interview

Meals provide a more relaxed atmosphere, and interviewees often chat, saying things that hurt their candidacy. Remember, this is still an interview—you are not speaking off the record. *All ears are listening to you.* Remain in your role and answer each question accordingly. Lengthier answers are okay, but never monopolize the conversation. Be aware of the interviewer's desire to learn about the *real* you. He or she will also watch your restaurant etiquette, so be polite to everyone you encounter, especially the waiter. Allow the interviewer to pay for the meal. Select an entrée that is easy to eat, not spaghetti or messy finger foods. Focus on the conversation and be cordial. I recommend you don't drink. This is a job interview. If you must drink, nurse something very slowly, leaving it half-touched. You need to remain sharp.

During these meetings, employers often try to uncover personality traits, outside interests, and personal information. Are you a good conversationalist? Would you interact well at company functions or client meetings? What are your personal circumstances? Are you single? Married? Do you have children? Are you divorced? Do you have time-consuming sports or hobbies?

To control this meeting, ask a lot of questions about the company, the duties of the job, and immediate challenges. A good, conversational question is to ask the interviewer about his or her job and why the company would be a good place to work. Throughout this interview, continually sell yourself and your ability to do the job.

Skype or Videoconferencing Interview

Many employers have turned to using Skype to interview candidates who don't live nearby. Colleges and universities are finding Skype (videoconferencing over the Internet) to be the perfect solution to meet job candidates no matter where they reside. Business professor Diane MacDonald at Pacific Lutheran University stated that many departments all over campus have been using Skype over the last few years. "We interview faculty candidates from all around the world," she said. "Skype interviews are held between the candidate and the search committee, so there may be as many as three to five people participating in the interview. Each one of the committee members has a say in whether someone will be offered a campus visit or not."

A senior Microsoft executive shared his experiences with me. "Microsoft uses Skype all the time. We interview senior people from all over the country, and sometimes internationally. In my group, we need people who are smart but also 'have a personality' and can interact with customers, partners, managers, and other executives. Therefore using Skype is tremendously useful to get a 'feel' of a candidate and a better understanding of their personality prior to bringing them in. It's also very cost-effective too," he explained.

One engineering client mentioned that inside his Fortune 100 manufacturer, it's common to have a Skype interview if you and the manager live in different regions. He got his promotion this way and never met the new boss in person until he started the job in one of the company's other locations.

Skype interviews can present a new challenge to the job hunter. Job candidates need to be comfortable using Skype and able to recover if there is a technical glitch in transmission. Appearing to be technically savvy is vital to making a good impression.

Skype Interview Dos and Don'ts

Ask in advance all the details about this format. Whom is it for? How long will the interview be? How many people will be there interviewing you? Don't expect the arranger to volunteer much, so ask and call back a second time if you need more clarification.

- Don't start out by apologizing for your unfamiliarity with using Skype. That is not what the employer wants to hear. Practice several times using this technology so you know how to connect, reconnect, adjust the volume, etc.

- Pay attention to what you are wearing; dress as you would if you were appearing in person. Select a conservative suit and be sure you do not have any plaids or bright print colors, as these don't look good when viewed via a monitor.
- Test the equipment and the place you plan to conduct the interview from in advance. Make sure the background is uncluttered and professional (not the kitchen or bedroom). Ensure that the space you are at is completely quiet and you will have no interruptions during the interview.
- Practice and get used to the camera and talking to your computer. Try not to move around a lot—nervousness and movements are magnified when you are on video. You must seem confident, comfortable, and enthusiastic about their job. Smile often—you will come across as a warmer, more likable person.
- Relax and rely on your preparation; use your 5 Point Agenda, your 60 Second Sell, and keep your answers under 60 seconds—with videoconferencing shorter answers are better.

Videotaping You

In one situation, the company videotapes the entire process. Often this is to "show" the candidates to management back at headquarters and to eliminate the expense of flying you to that location. Trainers and sales personnel are most likely to be asked to be videotaped. Often, a short presentation is required from you as part of this process. You are almost always told in advance about this type of format. Here are some guidelines:

- Ask in advance all the details about this format. Whom is it for? Where will the camera be? How long will the interview be? Are there any special presentations you will be asked to make? Call back if you need more clarification.
- Practice using a video camera to record a role-playing session or the presentation they intend to tape. Your movements and nervous actions are exaggerated on video. Watch that your nonverbal clues and facial expressions are smooth and not distracting.
- Get used to the camera. People can get very anxious, and the nervousness can take center stage if you don't relax. Practice in front of the camera until it no longer has any influence on you.
- Focus totally on the interviewer and forget the camera. Staring into the camera will just make you nervous and cause you to make mistakes.
- Your poise and self-confidence are being assessed here. Be sure to exude these traits.
- Smile often—when the tape is viewed, you will come across as a warmer, more likable person.

Fly-In/Relocation Interview

Usually you've had a screening interview prior to the company's deciding that it will fly you in for the next interview. Try to arrive the day before the actual interview. Many candidates are nervous wrecks when they arrive late, or just minutes before the interview is to start, because of late flights and poor directions. Usually, you will be too stressed or too tired to do your best, so try to plan to arrive the night before, even if you pay for the hotel yourself. These interviews often involve relocation, though occasionally it's just that the "head office" wants to see you before giving you the job in the region where you live. Relocation is a major decision, so think it through and research the potential town or city, cost of living, and quality of life.

A common mistake is to arrive at these interviews too overconfident, thinking, "They must really like me if they are covering all the costs to see me." Never assume the job is yours or that the interview is an expenses-paid vacation. These attitudes often lead to losing the position.

Some tips to remember:

- Know in advance who'll pay for expenses; typically, the company does. Be leery of companies that want you to cover all the costs and say they'll reimburse you. It could take months to get the money, if you ever get it at all.
- Ask the company to make the hotel reservation, keeping convenience to the company's location as the first priority.
- Place your interview outfit and all your job-search materials in carry-on luggage. You can't afford the embarrassment that lost luggage causes.
- It's usually acceptable to ask to stay on a day or two to check out the area. You might inquire if someone from the company could show you around. If you have children, ask HR for detailed information on schools and if any test results are available to separate poor schools from good ones. Look at apartments and houses and get prices so you have a more realistic idea of what it costs to live in the area.
- Watch expenses. Now is not the time to treat friends or order steak and lobster with expensive wine, running up big bills.
- Taxis, or a scheduled car service, are often an easier way for you to get around, especially in cities like L.A. or

D.C., where traffic is bad even when it's not rush hour. If you rent a car, get a map, with clear directions, even if you use a GPS. Always stop and ask if you are lost.

- Be safe. If you ever feel that the hotel is in a high-crime or unsafe area—move. Single women need to exercise caution, especially going anywhere in a new city alone at night.

- Show interest in both the city and the job. One candidate, interviewing at a prestigious law firm, lost the job when a partner asked, "So are you ready to leave San Francisco and move to Boston?" Her "I'm not sure" caused him to offer a more interested and committed candidate the job. Use this trip to closely evaluate: Can I live here? Would I like it? Would my family? Will it fast-track my career? Is it a good job? Does it pay well enough to maintain or improve my standard of living?

Testing Interview

Many companies hire outside consultants to help them develop a profile and determine each candidate's true skills, abilities, and personality traits. The consultant or HR person asks you to take a test—or several, for that matter. Among those you might encounter are:

- Math quiz
- Outlook email test
- Spelling quiz
- Personality test; e.g., Myers-Briggs
- Compatibility test
- Management style indicator
- Computer usage; e.g., Word or Excel
- In-box test

- Case study test with problems to solve
- Communications test examining writing skills
- Write and give a presentation

These tests can be short or last a day or two. They can make a candidate nervous—very nervous, since the pressure's on to perform well. Do your best and ask for clear directions. No one ever gets a perfect score during two days of assessment. But employers are seeking to validate your strengths and uncover your weaknesses, so be careful and thorough. Read directions twice and follow them exactly. Be sure to proofread answers, and pay attention to proper spelling and grammar.

One client sailed through day one of the personality test and an afternoon of replying to videotaped job problems: for example, angry customer, employee squabble, project with deadline, and missing work. It was the "in-box" procedure he felt he didn't do well on. Indeed he hadn't: the consultant's report labeled him "disorganized." With his dream job slipping away, he wrote his potential boss a detailed letter explaining how he organized his last complex job and projects. The employer questioned the accuracy of the testing (as hiring managers often do) and hired this client, who has since proven to be one of the best managers in the company.

Drug testing, credit, and criminal background checks are mandatory at some companies, for everyone at every level. For a drug test, be careful to list any medications you are taking. They can affect the results, so trying to hide your antidepressant prescription can cause a problem in the results and may end with you cited as a drug user. Privacy laws often require outside agencies to conduct the tests, but if you take medication daily, by all means tell the test giver about it. It is not necessary to mention it to the interviewer.

Beware of the Bizarre Interview

Over the years, I've heard of some very strange things that have happened during interviews, from the interviewer asking the candidate out on a date to, even worse, being propositioned as a prelude to getting the job. The list is long. My question to you is this: *why would you ever want to work for them?*

If a red flag goes up in your head when a potential employer gets bizarre, heed the warning and look elsewhere for the job of your dreams.

On the other hand, don't be that guy or that girl who makes the interviewer say, "That person was so strange." The president of a hospital system described the woman doctor who interviewed all day carrying a baby in a sling around her chest. The employer often was distracted and he questioned her judgment, commenting to the recruiter: "Some job candidates act clueless about how they present themselves. Bringing a baby to a job interview is likely the dumbest thing any professional could do. It bugged me all day. Needless to say we decided not to hire this lady doctor because of her poor judgment and arrogance that accommodating her was our prime objective."

One VP of HR mentioned a candidate for a chief-of-technology job who, while waiting in an open office for the CEO to enter for the final stage of his interview, spent the time clipping his nails. That sure got everyone's attention, but in the wrong way. It's key to stay at the top of your game so that other people make these weird mistakes, not you.

Negotiation Interview

The job offer has been made. You're now in control. The employer has changed hats and is eagerly attempting to get you to join his team. Use this time to learn about internal politics, the company's goals, and the role your position and decisions will play in the global scheme of the company. Ask about promotional tracks and training opportunities. Ask to meet your potential staff, and if you have not met the person who would be your boss, insist on it before you accept. You should now learn all about the benefits, and here's where you discuss and settle on an agreeable salary.

This interview can be vital to your assessment of the corporate culture. Frequently, people take the job when it is offered by phone. They start, and within a week they know they've made a terrible mistake. Often, a negotiation interview would have revealed potential conflicts, such as changes in benefits or job duties that differ from those mentioned at the first interview. One client was promised a necessary and highly desirable training program. At the negotiation interview that promise was changed: the training would be offered six months or so down the line. That training was vital to her success. When a few other things changed as well, she passed on the job.

There may be reasons to refuse a job. Ask, "Are there any problems, situations, or reasons that exist that could dissuade me from taking this job?" Never underestimate intense, political conflicts between employees you will manage. Get the facts and think the situation through thoroughly. Ask what changes upper management is making to resolve these personnel issues. Be leery if no one has plans to take control, especially when two battling employees have been at it for quite a while. Determine what kind of time, energy, and upper-management agenda will be needed to solve or stick with this potentially emotionally draining situation.

Last, ask if there was an internal candidate who did not get this job. Will you supervise that person? How will he or she react to you? Be concerned about how that candidate's workmates will interact and treat you. Be careful—these situations can often sabotage your ability to succeed in the new position.

Gather your facts, insights, and impressions during this time. Properly utilized, this interview allows you to select an organization where you really can leave each day saying, "I love my job."

Act as if it were impossible to fail and you never will.

CHAPTER 12

Pitfalls to Avoid

P art of our strategy for a successful interview is to have you avoid the mistakes that people often make. The twenty-one common errors you'll want to avoid are:

1. Being Late

Many employers feel that if you're late for the interview, you may never show up on time for your job. Need I say more? Get the directions, know how to get there and where to park, and give yourself more than enough time so that you will arrive early. Wait, collect your thoughts, and then open the employer's door about five minutes before the scheduled appointment.

2. Inappropriate Attire

Most people simply don't think about their appearance. They don't realize the importance of that first few seconds, when they meet the employer for the first time. The employer looks at you and, based on your appearance, decides whether or not you would fit in his organization. He decides not to hire you based solely on the way you're dressed and/or your personal hygiene. Whether you like it or not, it's human nature and it happens every day. The employer's immediate decision is based on whether you would be an appropriate person to *represent* the company. Remember, *you want to get the job*. Although many of us live in a business causal dress workplace, that doesn't mean you can be casual for the job interview. Nor is it the time to express your creative personality. Many people lose jobs because of their wild clothes, earrings, mismatched colors, greasy hair, dirty nails, and sloppiness. Put your best foot forward. After all, it is important that the interview *not* end the moment the interviewer sees you.

3. No Market Research

It's amazing how many people go to a job interview with no information about the company, no thought about the job they'll be doing, and no idea as to how they're going to relate their skills to the company's needs. The more inside information you can get, the more accurately you're going to be able to phrase your answers to demonstrate how your skills will fill the employer's needs. This is effective self-marketing. Spend the time to call contacts, read company literature, and go on the Internet to learn as much as possible about the employer's needs. Check out who their competitors are. This background information will help direct you in properly answering the interviewer's questions. It's imperative to your success. Many a candidate has not been hired because he appeared clueless about the company and how to meet its needs.

4. Assuming Your Resume Will Get You the Job

Do you believe that the employer diligently, and with a microscope, went through your resume and absorbed every single fact there? In reality, hiring managers have often merely glanced at the resume when they offer you an interview and will not have looked at it again until the moment you're in front of them. Remember, employers know that good resumes can be purchased. In fact, it's best to assume that your resume will *not* get you the job. You will be selling your skills throughout the entire interview. Don't say, "Oh, well, it's in my resume." Assume they *haven't read* your resume and say, "I've got ten years of experience in the graphic design field."

5. Believing the Person with the Best Education, Skills, and Experience Will Get the Job

This is not the case, based on my experience as a hiring employer and on discussions with numerous other employers. Sometimes the person who has the best experience, the best skills, and the best education doesn't feel like she'd fit into the organization. She just doesn't have the right personality or a cooperative attitude. Also, employers may become concerned that the candidate is overqualified and will leave too quickly. Whatever the reason, don't assume that top credentials are all it takes to get hired.

6. Failure to Prepare

This is a fatal error. I can't stress enough how important it is that you prepare prior to the interview. Write out answers to prospective questions. Analyze and prepare your 5 Point Agenda. Memorize your 60 Second Sell. Practice interview questions using a role-playing situation. Try a tape recorder or get feedback from another person. Advanced preparation makes you feel and sound confident about your abilities to do the job. It's crucial to your success.

7. Believing the Interviewer Is an Expert

This is a myth. Most managers hire only their own staff. Very few are skillfully trained in the techniques of conducting an interview. Those who do receive training often just get instructions on which questions are legal to ask. Don't assume that they'll know the direction the interview needs to go. Sometimes it's to your advantage to direct the conversation to effectively make your points.

8. Failure to Inspire Confidence

Interviews are not the time to be humble and meek. If you don't express competency and confidence that you can do the job, the employer will recognize that you probably *can't* do the job. Eye contact, a smile, and some enthusiasm in your voice are good covers for any nervousness you feel inside. Many employers have told me during reference checks, "She's really quite good at the job—it's too bad she interviews so poorly." Practice, practice, practice, and you will improve.

9. Failure to Demonstrate Skills

Many people will sit through the interview without clearly telling the employer what skills they'd bring to the job. They're quiet; their answers may be very general or very vague. Employers don't hire for vague generalities. They hire for specifics. Specific skills, past experience, examples of how you have done that kind of work before—specifics are what employers make decisions to hire on. Be sure to be detailed but concise whenever you answer.

10. Appearing Desperate or Highly Stressed Out

An unfortunate reality of hiring is that people are desperate. When you're an employer, interviewing somebody whose desperation keeps coming through often makes you feel sorry for the person, but you don't hire him. I've had many employers tell me, "You know, I really felt sorry for him," but when I asked, "Well, did you hire him?" they all said, "Well no, I didn't." The desperation turns them off. They're afraid that person doesn't want their particular job, he just wants *any* job. And to the employer, your wanting *their* job is what's most important. You want to appear as if there are other opportunities on your horizon. You may have to act; maybe you *are* desperate. But if you convey that desperation to the employer in the interview, it can hurt your chances of getting hired.

11. Mishandling Supplemental Questions or Tests

Some employers will ask you to fill out additional questionnaires or take a test during the hiring process. These must be taken seriously, so try to gather as much information as possible in advance to prepare thoroughly. Ask the organization for specific details on exactly what the tests or written supplemental questions will be about. Don't guess, *know*. Be sure to think carefully and to follow directions for all written answers. Proofread and be as careful as possible.

I've seen employers give equipment-simulation tests, typing tests, computer tests, written exams, personality tests, problems to solve, materials to proofread, work to analyze and prioritize, plus other tasks to determine hireability. Learn as much as you can and practice in advance. On the day of the interview, practice again, then do your best. Most errors come from making yourself too nervous, putting an exorbitant amount of pressure on yourself, or being unprepared. Some employers may want you to submit to a drug test. Do so. Your refusal will eliminate you as a candidate. If you take prescription medicine, inform the person conducting the test, to document the prescription.

12. Believing the Last Five Minutes Are the Most Important

Actually, the most important time is the first 60 seconds, when the interviewer makes the decision that she's going to listen to you. After that, you need to take every opportunity to demonstrate your skills and your abilities with proven examples of work you've done in the past. In reality, using *all* the time well is most important.

13. Thinking All References Are Created Equal

They are not. Some individuals, especially those who have previously worked with you, can aid you in being offered a position. Others can actually deter an employer from hiring you. When choosing references, consider testing them to find out exactly what they will say about you. Ask a friend to call and get a reference on you. Have that person report back. One client reported that when called for a reference her assistant took credit for organizing the office and thus the client came off in a less than favorable light. Needless to say, she dropped her assistant from her reference list.

Obtain permission from a reference in advance. Help them to be a good reference by writing a letter or sending them an email nicely reminding them about the experiences and abilities you'd like them to discuss. This letter often helps refresh their memories if it's been a while since you've worked together.

Under no circumstances use a boss who will say negative things. Find someone else who can talk about your strengths and contributions even if you were fired. After all, you select your references, so choose those names carefully. Be sure to check that all references' information—titles, addresses, phone numbers, emails—is correct so that the employer doesn't find the people on your list "no longer here."

14. Not Being the Ideal Worker

Employers want workers willing to be adaptable, to learn new skills, and to take on new tasks as needed. All jobs undergo change in some form or another. Demonstrate that you love to learn and are willing to do whatever is needed to help the department and company achieve its goals now and in the future.

15. Lying on the Resume or Application

Nearly one third of all job applicants have been caught lying about their education. Employers often check, so never misrepresent yourself—firing is almost always the result. Fudging the figure when asked to state your last salary on an application is also lying and will not be validated when your employer is called and asked, "Can you verify that Mary Brown's salary was $41,500?" You'll be in trouble if the answer is no. (Incidentally, all employers can do is validate—they won't reveal a salary figure when asked.) The best approach is to leave the salary request blank. Strive to state things in a positive manner but do so honestly, with integrity, expecting that the employer will check.

16. Your Nervousness Comes Across as Appearing Uninterested in the Job

Fear and intimidation often keep people from relaxing and performing well in an interview. They resort to a monotone voice that makes them seem to lack any enthusiasm for the job. Employers want you to *want* their job. Be friendly, smile, and ask good questions (see chapter 9 for help). If you don't act interested, the employer will hire someone else who does.

17. Bragging

Selling yourself effectively means giving examples that substantiate your claims. Bragging often comes from weak candidates' thinking they can snow the interviewer. You must be prepared to demonstrate *the results* of your sales ability, leadership, or whatever else you claim to be outstanding in. Results, specifics, and examples with substance are what will really influence an employer.

18. Giving Lengthy Answers

An interviewer's attention span will fade quickly, so don't bore him to death. One CFO commented, referring to a potential vice president's twenty-minute response to a question, "Wow, could you imagine that guy in a meeting? He'd never get to the point and we'd be there all day."

Best approach—keep the conversation moving by answering questions in less than 60 seconds.

19. Inability to Tolerate Pauses or Silence

The interviewer does not expect or need you to speak every second. When you finish answering a question, simply *tolerate* the silence while he or she absorbs your answer, takes notes, or formulates the next question. Don't babble on and on—you will appear nervous (because you are) and come across as a poor communicator. Be concise and thorough, and never take more than a minute with your response.

20. Leaving Your Cell Phone On

Nothing is more important than your conversation with the interviewer. Many employers complain that people check their phone and even take calls or do a text during their interview. That action pretty much guarantees you'll not get the job. Turn your phone to OFF so you won't have any distractions during your interview.

21. Thinking Your Major Goal Is to Get the Job

Really? I thought your major goal is to find out about the job—to learn what the company's needs are and to determine if your skills and abilities fit their needs. Would this be a good marriage, uniting your skills and abilities with their job's needs, and bringing you both together? That's really what you're looking for. During the interview you are investigating them just as they are investigating you. Realize it's an exchange out of which both of you will decide if this is a possible fit and a good job for you. Use the time to gather decision-making information to aid you in determining whether this is a position in which you'll be able to contribute, be productive, and enjoy going to work.

Always do your best.
It is your constant effort
to be first-class
in everything you attempt
that will make you conquer
the heights of excellence and success.

CHAPTER 13

The Spotlight Is on You

In every interview you are an actor. Your role is the job seeker. Just as Hollywood's top stars practice and prepare, so should you. Every actor knows that spoken words are enhanced by body language, facial expressions, voice intonations, and props. When the job interview's spotlight shines on you, you begin a one-time-only performance. So make your words, body language, and voice work to aid you in landing the job.

Dealing with Nervousness

Important events where we are judged and need to perform well can make anyone nervous. A little nervousness can actually help you be sharp and on your toes, and improve your performance. A heart-thumping, face-twitching, voice-quivering nervousness will reflect poorly on you and the strong, self-confident, "I can solve your problems" impression you are trying to make. Try these techniques to lessen your nervousness.

Technique 1

Visualize success. See yourself smiling and happy. In your mind, create a picture of the employer's eyes glued to you, hanging on every word. Hear her say, "I want you for the job." Believe that you will be successful, liked, and wanted in this encounter. Your state of mind directly affects your performance. Focus only on confidence-building thoughts.

Technique 2

Listen to a motivational tape or watch an inspiring YouTube video shortly before the interview. The confidence and morale-boosting words will give you needed moral support and decrease your apprehensions.

Technique 3

Rid your body of nervous tension. Just before you go into the interview, find a private spot outside or in the restroom and shake each leg. Then shake both arms and hands. The physical exercise releases the tension that has built up, and relaxes you.

Technique 4

Take deep breaths. As your hand reaches for the door, take a couple of deep breaths, slowly breathing in and out. Think of a calm and beautifully peaceful scene to help you relax a bit.

These four techniques will help to decrease your nervousness. And practice makes perfect. All the preparation creating answers, and your 60 Second Sell, should reassure you that you are prepared and will do your best.

What to Bring

The night before the interview, pack up what you need to bring. Always have extra resumes—yes, they do lose them and misplace them. Bring your list of references. Be sure all addresses, emails, and phone numbers are current and accurate. Include any work samples and the list of questions you intend to ask. Carry your research, the list of those questions you want answered, your 5 Point Agenda, and your 60 Second Sell. You'll want to review all of these an hour or two before entering the interview to keep the ideas fresh in your mind. Include a notepad and pen in case you need them.

Decide if you will carry a briefcase or a simple leatherbound notebook holder into the interview. Organize your materials, and you are ready to go. Be careful not to have too many things—briefcase, notepad binder, materials, cell phone, purse—all in your hands. Combine and compact into one easily carried piece, two maximum. And always turn off your cell phone before you enter the interview.

First Impressions

First impressions are difficult to change. Before you even say hello, the employer's mind is evaluating attire, hygiene, and style, formulating an opinion, because what you wear sends powerful signals. The impression must be positive or it could eliminate your chances of getting the job. Select a suit that is conservative but modern. Be certain it is clean and fits well, and pay careful attention to the details. Smile at everyone you meet. As you introduce yourself to the receptionist, smile and take a moment to ask her name. Be sure to add that you are glad to meet her. When the interviewer approaches, stand, smile, and offer a firm handshake. Nothing creates a poorer impression than a weak, couple-of-fingers shake. Start out exuding confidence; the smile and firm handshake are key.

Nonverbal Clues

Employers evaluate what they hear, while giving credence to what they see. Nervous gestures, such as playing with your hair, looking away when you are asked questions, playing with a pen, or tapping your fingers, can absorb their attention. Nervous job hunters then compensate by crossing their arms, a gesture that radiates a closed, unapproachable, "Stay away from me" message. To demonstrate that you are relaxed and confident, sit with your hands on your lap, or rest them open on the table if one is in front of you. Equally acceptable is to open your notepad and hold a pen.

Your movements, gestures, posture, and facial expressions are an important part of your overall performance. A sincere smile sends a warm, confident message. Eye contact is one of the important things employers notice about you. It is crucial and conveys that your message is believable. We all get suspicious of a person who focuses his eyes on the floor, or to the side, but rarely on us. Practice until it is second nature to look *at* the person when answering a question.

Your face can reflect so many expressions—humor, confidence, seriousness, concern, enthusiasm—all of which add depth and meaning to your words. Be sure not to sit there stoically, with a blank face. You will fail to appear "real" and come across as boring and dull. If you sit rigid, upright, or frozen, you communicate anxiety and insincerity. Likewise, slouching projects cowardliness, insecurity, and less competence. Sit up tall, but lean forward or use your hands from time to time to make your point and draw in your listener.

Use vocal intonations to make your point. Pauses, soft tones, and louder tones all add interest to a conversation. One department head commented that she listens to applicants' tone. If they are long-winded, monotonic, and boring, she eliminates them. After all, she is the one who will constantly be listening to them in meetings. She, like many employers, wants someone confident, human, more personable. This does not mean loud and boisterous. Quiet introverts often excel in interviews because they project a quiet, confident self. Be yourself, be natural, but use these nonverbal techniques to project a more appealing image to the employer.

Show-and-Tell

Proof. Every employer loves to see evidence that you can do the job. Just as a graphic designer never interviews without a portfolio of her work, you need to bring samples that demonstrate your abilities to do the job.

This can be a very powerful tool that few ever use. When a client was trying to change fields to advance his career, he faced many roadblocks. A friend helped him get an interview with a large company for his dream job. I had him bring in his laptop so he could demonstrate his skills as a project manager by showing some of the sophisticated spreadsheets and tracking systems he had created. From the moment they began to see his work, the interviewers changed. He could see it in their body language, and later said, "I knew I had them." Indeed, the work samples actually *showed* the potential this client had, and so the rest of the interview focused on his show-and-tell pieces. It was bringing in these samples that really turned the interview his way, and indeed he got this great job, with a very significant raise too.

Show-and-tell examples may be a form you developed that sped up production, articles you have written, materials you have created, webpages you've laid out, brochures that list you as a panelist or speaker, work-related spreadsheets, budgets, or drawings or illustrations you've sketched. Bring in anything that clearly demonstrates how you have done the job before. In fact, one chef brought in samples of his best dessert; he was hired right after everyone tasted it. Remember, seeing is often believing and a picture or, in this case, a paper, journal, brochure, report, etc., brings your words to life in a very impressive and influential way.

Field Knowledge

Potential bosses are trying to determine how much you know in your field of expertise, be it human resources, network systems, marketing, electrical engineering, fund-raising, payroll, etc. The higher up your job, the more depth of knowledge you need to have. One CEO said, "I expect my top people to be an inch wide but a mile deep in their area of expertise." Read up on trends. Notice industry changes and current problems, so as to be nimble in discussing your position and the field in which your work is done. Visit your professional association's website to acquaint yourself with current issues being discussed. Become well versed in the products, services, and operations of the company you are interviewing with. If you educate yourself before the interview, you can make a very appealing package and cross over into new and very different fields or companies. Never go to the interview without doing this important homework. Every applicant must also stress his or her interest in the field, commitment to stay up on changes, and desire to learn new skills to better perform the job.

When a person is trying to change careers, the employer often dreads all the time that will be needed to teach that person about the field. To prevent this from becoming a hiring obstacle, especially if you are trying to change fields, be self-taught. Read books and articles on the new field you want to enter. Talk with successful people who hold jobs similar to the one you want. Learn the field's jargon and familiarize yourself with the future trends and what impact they might have. Acquire the needed background to eliminate the employer's concern that you know *nothing* about the field. Use this self-acquired knowledge in the interview.

60-Second Work Example

Using examples is the best way to communicate clearly—to paint a picture that allows the employer to see you doing similar tasks, successfully, for her. Predetermined work examples are a very effective tool you can bring to the interview. You'll never flounder and search for an example. Preselection allows you to slowly sift through your background and extract the right situation to make your point. Prepare examples that demonstrate each point in your 5 Point Agenda. Prepare examples that deal with problem solving, supervisory style, teamwork ability, and planning and organizational skills, especially if your job deals with projects and deadlines. These examples or stories need to be introduced, told, then summarized in no more than 60 seconds. Advance preparation allows you to use these examples to answer questions appropriately.

If you are asked a question about dealing with employee performance or problem solving, you could try an example like this: "Solving problems is an important part of my work. At Northwest Hospital I had a staff person who was overwhelmed with her regular workload and trying to learn our new software. Everything was getting behind. I sat her down and we talked about the problem. Laura found it very hard to concentrate if there were any distractions as she began to apply what she'd been taught in the computer-training class. We decided that she could spend one hour each day for two weeks with her door closed and her phone forwarded to voice mail. We determined specific goals she needed to reach to master the new software so she could get the department back up to speed. I encouraged her daily, and she did make the needed progress. In fact, she surpassed all my expectations and within two months really improved our productivity with her new skills. I think it was the effort I made getting her input and help in finding an acceptable solution that encouraged and motivated her to try harder." When you offer specific details you make the employer think, "Yes, that's what we need." Using examples, you'll go a long way toward being hired.

Highlight Transferable Skills

Many of the abilities you develop for one employer will be equally valuable to another. These "transferable skills" build a fuller picture for the employer to consider.

You possess many skills that you fail to recognize but that an employer will see as necessary and important. At the top of most employers' lists are *computer skills*—highly valued from one employer to another. Here are other skill areas to consider. Select those that are important in doing the employer's job well and incorporate them into your answers and examples.

- **Managerial Skills.** Set goals, see the big picture, solve problems, handle details, plan projects, analyze, find resources, work well with others, obtain maximum productivity from others, gain cooperation, implement changes, supervise others, plan workflow, mediate staff conflicts, delegate, think globally.
- **Organizational/Planning Skills.** Structure events,

coordinate people and details, organize tracking or filing systems, set timelines, forecast, determine priorities, manage all aspects of large or multiple projects, develop alternatives, determine resources, solve problems, see the big picture and all the interacting components too, pay attention to the tiniest details, gather support and cooperation from others.

- **Communication Skills.** Exchange ideas, use probing questions to determine needs of others, sell products/services/ideas, persuade others to do what you want, use humor, tell stories, entertain others, write messages that clearly get across your meaning, teach or train, make impassioned pleas, edit comprehensive reports/proposals, express creativity, use vocabulary/grammar/language skills effectively, edit reports/publications, make speeches.

- **Leadership Skills.** Lead, motivate others, cause change, make decisions, be a visionary, forecast, recognize opportunities, praise others, direct projects and individuals.

- **Customer-Service Skills.** Meeting client/customer needs, troubleshooting, resourceful problem solving, courteous manner, listening, helpful attitude.

- **Financial Skills.** Budgets, cost spreadsheets, forecasting, modeling, price comparisons, negotiate better deals, notice cost-cutting or profit-making opportunities, cash management, using charts/graphs to make points, stretching a dollar, financial analysis.

- **Analytical Skills.** Using computers, knowledge about system networks, skill in a specific software, research, analyze data, interpret results, organize large volumes of information, evaluate options considering pros/cons and consequences, design efficient systems, collect and process information in user-friendly form, diagnose

problems, determine workable solutions, seek more
efficient procedures, produce technical reports/surveys
or questionnaires, investigate, make new discoveries,
implement new systems, test new ideas/processes/
procedures/systems.
- **Interpersonal Skills.** Counseling, negotiations,
listening, empathy, sensitivity to others, rapport
builder, deal effectively with conflicts, social interactor,
help others, share ideas, solve problems, adviser,
mediator, bring people together, collaborator.

Handling Small Employers

In the next decade, according to the Department of Labor, job
growth will increase by the greatest degree among small employers, particularly organizations with fewer than one hundred people. This presents a dilemma to the job seeker, because
often very little information about the employer is available
prior to the interview. To aid in your preparation, try to obtain
as much information from the person who arranges the interview or someone else in the office. Ask what their website address is. When asking a few questions, if you get, "Oh, they'll
cover that," you'll need to use your best guess and prepare. As
you start the interview, use this technique to gain the necessary
information and reorganize your answers to address their spoken needs. Simply say, "Mr. Employer, *before we get started*,
could you tell me in more detail about the day-to-day responsibilities?" Then ask, "What do you consider the priorities? Is
there any special training or experience you're seeking?" Be
sure to use the phrase "before we get started"—it allows you to
gain insight, and the employer believes he hasn't begun yet
even though this information will help you frame your answers.

From those few questions, you will learn what important

ingredients this employer desires. You can address his needs by quickly editing your 60 Second Sell. You may need to adapt on the spot, but you've gotten the insights and can now stress your strengths to meet his needs, while most other candidates will be operating blind.

Listen

Hear their questions; *hear* their needs; *hear* their expectations. If you listen carefully, employers often reveal everything you need to know.

Often, job hunters just don't listen. It is frustrating to the interviewer to ask questions that never get answered. So listen closely. Many employers reveal their "hidden agendas," those few things that really influence their decision, if you listen closely to the questions they ask and the information they offer. I recently interviewed four people in order to hire a program coordinator. I told each candidate that computer skills were important. One person emphasized her organizational abilities, another her attention to detail and willingness to do whatever was asked. A third repeatedly discussed her computer abilities but never addressed the fact that my company was using different software. The gentleman I hired spoke about his computer abilities and brought along sample flyers, documents, and even a newsletter he'd done. He met my most important criterion—good computer skills. The others never heard me. As the potential employer, I told them, but they didn't listen. If they had, one of them might have gotten the job. Instead, he did!

The only people who fail
are those who do not try.
All your dreams can come true
if you have the courage to pursue them.
The bigger you dream
the more you will achieve.

CHAPTER 14

The Convincing Close

Most employers use some sort of rating system at the end of an interview. Some may just jot down notes; others use a comprehensive evaluation form. With this in mind, be aware that the way you end the interview will be a vital component in securing the job offer.

Be Memorable: End with Your 60 Second Sell

Most seasoned interviewers will tell you that it is easy to forget a person 60 seconds after she runs out the door. You can often sit back at the end of the day, look at the resumes, and wonder who was who.

Using the 60 Second Sell and the 5 Point Agenda ensures repetition of your major strengths. Creating examples that demonstrate these strengths and effectively answering questions in less than 60 seconds will reinforce your abilities and your desire to do the job. Using your 60 Second Sell as you are ending the interview will leave the employer with those few thoughts to ponder as she fills out her evaluation form, remembering your five most marketable skills to meet her company's needs and do the job.

The end has come; the employer has asked all her questions, and you've followed with yours. You've learned about the next stage and when the company will be making a decision. Just before you get up to leave, close with your 60 Second Sell. Be sure to incorporate any major point that you learned from the employer during the interview, replacing one of the original five points with a new one to hit upon the organization's need. Here's how one client won the job:

"Thank you for the opportunity to meet with you and learn about your needs for an executive director. Let me just summarize what I would bring to this job. I believe my thirteen years in association management, assisting associations in their development and growth, would be an asset to you. It sounds as if I'd be able to put to use all the event planning and the media contacts I've developed to create very profitable events, obtaining the publicity and corporate sponsors that ensure high attendance. I believe the addition of seminars and workshops would be a new revenue source for you, as it was for my last employer. Finally, I think my resourcefulness in being innovative, maximizing the use of volunteers, and working with restricted budgets would be very beneficial in achieving your goals. I believe I would make some very valuable contributions if I joined your team. Thank you again for this meeting and your interest."

Format the close to directly apply your abilities to what the employer has revealed about the position. Once said, stand, shake hands, and leave.

Employer Rating Chart

As soon as the door closes, the employer takes notes. She decides whether or not you are someone she could work with. Below is a typical ratings report an employer might complete after each interview. Note that this employer uses facts and impressions she's gathered during the interview process. First the determination—*can you do the job*—evaluating technical competency, noting weaknesses and strengths. Skill areas are examined; job knowledge, communication skills, managerial style, organizational/planning, problem-solving, and decision-making abilities are rated. Next they make a determination on how willing you seem to perform the duties. Finally the hiring manager or interviewer determines if you would be easy to manage based on what he's heard and seen. A decision is made about whether you are a potential candidate to be hired for the job. See the chart on pages 188 and 189.

Post-interview Assessment

Immediately after the interview, find a spot to sit down and write out your assessment of the employer and the position. This will help you to improve your interviews in the future and to evaluate the employer's needs for future interviews if the process continues; also, note any special problems or tough questions to practice answering in the future. Jot down the following:

- Description of job duties
- Impression of the potential workplace
- Impression of your future boss
- Concerns or weak areas you might have in performing this job
- Training time to get up to speed
- Unanswered questions or concerns you'll need further clarification on
- Tough questions you found hard to answer
- Rate your performance
- Note any areas where you might try to improve
- Are you interested in the job? The company?

Interview Evaluation

Name: _____

Position: _____

Technical competency:
Candidate's strongest skills are:
1. _____
2. _____
3. _____

Compared to our job needs, these strengths are:
___ Not important ___ Somewhat important ___ Important

Performance of technical skills at previous job:
___ Poor ___ Below average ___ Adequate ___ Good ___ Excellent

Weaknesses or areas of concern:_____
_____

Overall job knowledge:
___ Poor ___ Below average ___ Adequate ___ Good ___ Excellent

Oral communication skills:
___ Poor ___ Below average ___ Adequate ___ Good ___ Excellent

Written communication skills:
___ Poor ___ Below average ___ Adequate ___ Good ___ Excellent

Organizational/planning abilities:
___ Poor ___ Below average ___ Adequate ___ Good ___ Excellent

Managerial skills:
Describe candidate's supervisory style: _____
_____

Rate style in relation to managing employees who will report to this person:
____ Poor ____ Below average ____ Adequate ____ Good ____ Excellent

Computer skills:
Hardware experience: _____
Software experience: _____
Training needed: _____

Decision-making experience:
____ Poor ____ Below average ____ Adequate ____ Good ____ Excellent

Interpersonal/customer skills:
____ Poor ____ Below average ____ Adequate ____ Good ____ Excellent

Analytical abilities:
____ Poor ____ Below average ____ Adequate ____ Good ____ Excellent

Work ethic:
____ Poor ____ Below average ____ Adequate ____ Good ____ Excellent

Personality:
Describe: _____
_____

Asset for the job:
____ No ____ Yes ____ Most definitely
Comments: _____
_____

Hiring rating:
____ Definitely not ____ Adequate with some reservations
____ Possible hire ____ Definitely hire
Explanation: _____
_____

Signature: _____
Date: _____

Thank-you Notes

Employers can be influenced once you have left the room. A thank-you note can often reaffirm that they have made the right choice. The note can tip the hand in your favor if the choice is between you and someone else. The employer believes a person who really wants the job is likely to perform better on the job. I recommend your note be on a card with the words "Thank You" printed on it in a professional, businesslike style (these are available from a local drugstore or card shop). Or choose plain, high-quality note card stationery that looks professional and expensive. Jot down a few lines, thanking the employer for the opportunity and reiterating a strength or two you would bring as a "valuable contributor to their team." Many seminar students want me to approve sending a simple email. No—they are forgotten five seconds after they are opened. The note—handwritten (print if your writing is not legible)—is a *personal* communication. Demonstrate the extra effort you put into your work. It certainly won't negatively affect your chances. Most candidates *do not* send thank-you notes. Here again is the chance to move to the top and be reevaluated. Notes must be mailed within twenty-four hours, preferably the same day as the interview if timing allows. Be sure to ask the hiring manager for her business card so you will have the correct address to mail your note to.

How to Remain a Viable Candidate
When Someone Else Gets the Job

Up to 15% of all new hires do not work out within the first two months. The reasons vary—perhaps the candidate continued interviewing and got a better offer, or his performance and personality did not fit the employer's needs.

One candidate accepted a position for a top management position. Relocation was involved, so the employer agreed to wait eight weeks for the candidate to start. On the night before he was scheduled to start, a fax arrived saying the person had changed his mind and wasn't coming.

There are times when *follow-up can win you the job.* Here's what to do:

1. Call to verify that the employer selected another candidate. Reiterate that you are still interested in the job if the person doesn't work out, and ask the employer to reconsider you if that should happen. A few of my clients ended up with the job simply because they did this and made it easy for the employer to call them again.

Don't burden the employer with questions about what you did wrong—he is not likely to honestly share that information. And never argue or get defensive. The employer will hire the person he feels is best suited for the job. A great technique, which many clients have had success using, is to inquire whether the company has any other available positions that you might qualify for. If so, secure the name of the hiring manager and contact that person at once. It's also a good idea to ask, "I'm sorry it didn't work out, Bill; by chance do you know of any other companies looking for a (use the job title you interviewed for) like me?" This has led savvy job hunters to their next new position.

2. Check back in four to six weeks to see if the person is working out. If he isn't, the employer will be very glad to hear from you.

3. Forget your pride. Pride does not pay your bills. Perhaps you didn't get the initial offer because you didn't sell yourself as effectively as you could have. Whether you are second, third, or fifth choice does not matter if in the end you're the one who *takes* the job and goes home with the paycheck. Be humble if you are called back, and resell the employer on your abilities to do his job well.

You will not salvage every lost opportunity. But so few candidates ever practice good follow-up techniques that you will be among scant competition if you do. And under the right circumstances *you* will grab the job from the jaws of defeat and get the position you really want.

Within you at this moment
is the power to do things
you never dreamed possible.

You know what you are today
but not what you may be tomorrow.

Always look at things as they can be.

You can do anything you wish to do,

have anything you wish to have,

be anything you wish to be.

When you do all the things
you are capable of
you will literally astound yourself.

CHAPTER 15

60 Seconds & You're Hired!

Real people use these techniques every day. They report that the 60 Second Sell and the 5 Point Agenda were instrumental in landing the job, and easy to create and use. They refer to them as great hiring shortcuts. Seminar participants sigh with relief once they learn my strategies for handling tricky, tough questions using effective, concise answers. Book readers email me about their successes. Clients repeatedly secure more money when they apply my salary-negotiation guidelines. Thousands have used these strategies, and they all have had the same conclusion—the strategies really work. That's why I'm convinced they will work for you.

Let me share a few success stories. No, not the easy cases. I selected the hard ones, those with real-life challenges that you could also be facing, to prove these techniques *land* jobs. Our real people include:

Tom—a laid-off, highly paid senior executive
Patricia—a professional who wanted to change fields
Jeff—a new college grad facing a very competitive job
    market
Linda—handling a divorce and a job change

Steve—wanted a promotion but lacked a degree
Janet—a return-to-work mom
David—an engineer who had a disability and had been
    laid off
Mary—an association director who was fired
Nicole—who wanted a promotion

Tom was a talented chief financial officer who had been highly paid before his company sold the broadcasting business whose financial operations he oversaw. Headhunters had told Tom he was overpaid and needed to expect a $20,000 salary cut. Tom's resume and targeted cover letter got him an interview with one of the country's top communications companies. This employer conducted nine hours of interviews with Tom over several meetings. Tom felt that the 5 Point Agenda helped him to demonstrate his abilities beyond his financial skills, including his team-development, strategic-planning, and presentation abilities. The short, 60-second answers really got the conversation going. He landed the job and got a better salary package than he had before by using our negotiation guidelines. Within one year, Tom was promoted to director of finance.

Patricia, a project manager, wanted to change fields. She was fascinated with software development, but all her experience had been in the retail industry. She spent hours researching this new field. She wrote to say it was her 60 Second Sell and my advice on answering tough questions that helped her to land her dream job. She's now happily employed as a project manager for a growing software company.

Jeff found that a business degree from a good four-year college was not as marketable as he thought it would be. On graduation day no one was standing in line to hire him. He was discouraged by how difficult the job hunt was and how long it was taking him. He had worked construction jobs to help pay for his college education and thus had no applicable experience to land his goal—a position in store management. Jeff and I worked on creating a 5 Point Agenda and a 60 Second Sell that demonstrated his strong work ethic and his ability to work well with all kinds of people. He was amazed that he indeed had important skills to sell an employer. He worked hard developing great answers to potential questions. Jeff was hired as an assistant store manager for a national paint store. His years in construction helped him to excel in his new career—selling house paint.

Linda was going through a difficult divorce when she got a notice that her employer was closing the branch office where she worked. Her situation was desperate—as the sole supporter of her children, she needed a job. Linda had had ten interviews and had failed miserably at each prior to our working together.

Linda and I evaluated her strengths. We created her 5 Point Agenda and 60 Second Sell and also created answers to difficult questions. We also worked on her demeanor and confidence. After two more interviews, Linda was hired as a loan officer at one of America's top banks.

Steve had been trained as a healthcare professional but found it hard to get promoted. He had been a successful nurse with an associate's degree as an RN, but a move into administration had eluded him primarily because he lacked a four-year college degree—nurses with bachelor's degrees continually beat him out. I stressed that he must use his leadership skills and not allow the employer to focus on his missing education. He had taken several management courses available through the hospital where he worked, plus he had volunteer management experience and had led committees and internal teams. Once he correctly started adding this experience into his 60 Second Sell, everything changed. Next time out, he landed an administrator's job and also negotiated an impressive salary.

Janet had had a successful communications career working

in media buying before she started having children. She stayed out of the workplace until her youngest turned twelve. Fifteen years is a long time to be absent from any field. I had her conduct informational interviews and do a complete skills analysis. She also went to the local community college for some crash computer classes to update and advance her skills. She did have a talent for understanding how advertising must align with marketing to influence sales and was excellent at handling customers. She got an assistant position to a sales manager who oversaw e-commerce and all print and broadcast media. Her ability to build positive customer relationships and solve problems quickly earned her a significant raise within the first few months on the job.

David lost his position as a manufacturing engineer due to downsizing and panicked because he knew employers often shy away from workers with a disability. Partially blind, he came to me by referral. We worked hard to cover any obstacles an employer might have. I recommended he immediately address how he overcame his disability in the workplace with a special computer keyboard that he provided and special magnifying eyeglasses. He also brought samples of his past work and excellent performance reviews he'd received in the past. We role-played answering questions and sent him out to interview with two new employers. Both offered him a job. He was pleasantly surprised. David started a new position having negotiated a salary increase and an extra week's vacation.

After she was fired, Mary underestimated how difficult her job search would be. She bombed during her first interview, easily tripping over the "Why were you let go?" questions. Mary secretly worried about whether she was as good as she thought. She feared landing a new position with the type of difficult politics that had been her downfall in her last job. We analyzed Mary's strengths as an association executive director—media, PR, events, conferences, interpersonal abilities, organization, and planning. Her weaknesses were budgets, finance, and trying to please everyone, especially board members with opposing agendas. Our coaching sessions restored her self-confidence—I knew she would work again and often told her so. We created a 5 Point Agenda and 60 Second Sell that emphasized her strengths. She investigated the associations to learn which environments offered opportunities to use her strengths, while not relying on her to provide the financial direction she was not skilled at. Last, she sought an organization with only one boss where she could achieve the goals that one person set out. She feels that using these techniques allowed her to be selected for an executive director position from among 155 candidates. She's been very successful and happy in her new position.

Nicole spent several years at a Fortune 500 company. She continued to take on new human resources duties as her job kept expanding. She had been promised a promotion to assistant director, but the title change and better salary never materialized. Although she performed a management job, her salary remained stuck. Fed up, she began to hunt for a job. In an early interview she told a hiring manager her true salary. The HR recruiter was a friend and confided to her later that once the hiring manager heard the low figure her current employer paid her, the employer changed his opinion of her and her achievements and abilities. (His job paid twice her salary.) During a coaching session, Nicole learned the correct salary negotiation techniques that are outlined in this book. She applied them when an impressive high-tech company needed a new human resources generalist. With good answers and solid work examples as well, she landed the job at a pay raise of 151% over the job she quit.

I've shared my shortcuts and hiring strategies to aid you in communicating to the employer how you can meet his or her needs. That is the key to open your door of opportunity. Just as these clients and countless others have found good positions, so will you. The 5 Point Agenda is an easy tool to create. It provides you with a clear direction to stress your five major strengths, demonstrating how well you can do the employer's job. The 60 Second Sell is a clever strategy that effectively markets your most important abilities in a short, concise way. It is also a powerful tool to use in closing an interview, leaving a strong, positive impression behind. You can now write out answers that, once spoken, will convince the employer to hire you. You know exactly how to negotiate for more salary and benefits in a way that produces results. All you need to do now is put these techniques into action. You can and will succeed. I know it's just 60 seconds and *you're* hired.

More Career Help Is Available

Career Counseling Services:

Robin offers telephone consultations, assisting clients worldwide, *anytime* and *anywhere* with interviewing, resume writing, cover letters, career changing, job search, and salary negotiations. For more info go to www.RobinRyan.com, email her at Robin@robin ryan.com, or call her office at (425) 226-0414.

Job Search Success Subscription Service:

Robin's innovative online program offers you a comprehensive way to access the best job hunting advice available. It encompasses all aspects of the job search along with vital motivation to propel you to land your new job faster. Learn more at www.RobinRyan .com.

Books and Audio CDs:

Robin's books are available online and in bookstores. These include:

- *Over 40 & You're Hired!*
- *Soaring on Your Strengths*
- *Winning Resumes,* second edition
- *Winning Cover Letters,* second edition
- *What to Do with the Rest of Your Life*

e-Newsletter:
Featuring Robin's career-advice column. Sign up FREE on
her homepage at www.RobinRyan.com.

Seminars and Workshops:
Robin is available to speak to groups, associations,
companies, and colleges. Contact her at Robin@
robinryan.com or visit her website.

Contact Robin Ryan at **(425) 226-0414**
Email her at Robin@robinryan.com
Visit her website at **www.RobinRyan.com**

AVAILABLE FROM PENGUIN

Over 40 and You're Hired!

Secrets to Landing a Great Job

Whether the economy is up or down, the job market is tough territory if you are over forty. America's top career counselor, Robin Ryan, offers her market-tested program that shows how to stand out effectively and appeal to employers.

Soaring On Your Strengths

Discover, Use, and Brand Your Best Self for Career Success

Robin Ryan's savvy, groundbreaking book is designed to help readers take advantage of a paradigm shift in the work place, with advice on self-promotion, relationship building, branding, and identifying your most marketable qualitites.

**PENGUIN
BOOKS**